W9-BOG-184

IN SEARCH

of the

SAVIOR

The Gospel of Mark

STUDY GUIDE
VOLUME 2

DR. DAVID JEREMIAH

with Dr. David Jeremiah

© 2018 Turning Point for God
P.O. Box 3838
San Diego, CA 92163
All Rights Reserved

Edited by Jordan Davis
Unless otherwise indicated, Scripture verses quoted are taken from the NEW KING JAMES VERSION.

Printed in the United States of America.

Contents

About
Dr. David Jeremiah
and Turning Point

D r. David Jeremiah is the founder of Turning Point, a ministry committed to providing Christians with sound Bible teaching relevant to today's changing times through radio and television broadcasts, audio series, books, and live events. Dr. Jeremiah's common-sense teaching on topics such as family, prayer, worship, angels, and biblical prophecy forms the foundation of Turning Point.

David and his wife, Donna, reside in El Cajon, California, where he serves as the senior pastor of Shadow Mountain Community Church. David and Donna have four children and twelve grandchildren.

In 1982, Dr. Jeremiah brought the same solid teaching to San Diego television that he shares weekly with his congregation. Shortly thereafter, Turning Point expanded its ministry to radio. Dr. Jeremiah's inspiring messages can now be heard worldwide on radio, television, and the Internet.

Because Dr. Jeremiah desires to know his listening audience, he travels nationwide holding ministry events that touch the hearts and lives of many people. According to Dr. Jeremiah, "At some point in time, everyone reaches a turning point; and for every person, that moment is unique, an experience to hold onto forever. There's so much changing in today's world that sometimes it's difficult to choose the right path. Turning Point offers people an understanding of God's Word as well as the opportunity to make a difference in their lives."

Dr. Jeremiah has authored numerous books, including *Escape the Coming Night* (Revelation), *The Handwriting on the Wall* (Daniel), *Overcoming Loneliness, Prayer—the Great Adventure, God in You* (Holy Spirit), *When Your World Falls Apart, Slaying the Giants in Your Life, 31 Days to Happiness—Searching for Heaven on Earth, Captured by Grace, Signs of Life, What in the World Is Going On?, The Coming Economic Armageddon, I Never Thought I'd See the Day!, God Loves You: He Always Has—He Always Will, Revealing the Mysteries of Heaven, Agents of the Apocalypse,* and *The God You May Not Know.*

How to Use This Study Guide

The purpose of this Turning Point study guide is to reinforce Dr. David Jeremiah's dynamic, in-depth teaching and to aid the reader in applying biblical truth to his or her daily life. This study guide is designed to be used in conjunction with Dr. Jeremiah's *In Search of the Savior—The Gospel of Mark, Volume 2* audio series, but it may also be used by itself for personal or group study.

Structure of the Lessons

Each lesson is based on one of the messages in the *In Search of the Savior—The Gospel of Mark, Volume 2* compact disc series and focuses on specific passages in the Bible. Each lesson is composed of the following elements:

- *Outline*

The outline at the beginning of the lesson gives a clear, concise picture of the topic being studied and provides a helpful framework for readers as they listen to Dr. Jeremiah's teaching.

- *Overview*

The overview summarizes Dr. Jeremiah's teaching on the passage being studied in the lesson. Readers should refer to the Scripture passages in their own Bibles as they study the overview. Unless otherwise indicated, Scripture verses quoted are taken from the New King James Version.

- *Personal and Group Application Questions*

This section contains a variety of questions designed to help readers dig deeper into the lesson and the Scriptures, and to apply the lesson to their daily lives. For Bible study groups or Sunday school classes, these questions will provide a springboard for group discussion and interaction.

- *Did You Know?*

This section presents a fascinating fact, historical note, or insight that adds a point of interest to the preceding lesson.

Personal Study

Thank you for selecting *In Search of the Savior—The Gospel of Mark, Volume 2* for your current study. The lessons in this study guide were created to help you gain fresh insights into God's Word and develop new perspectives on topics you may have previously studied. Each lesson is designed to challenge your thinking, and help you grow in your knowledge of Christ. During your study, it is our prayer that you will discover how biblical truth affects every aspect of your life and your relationship with Christ will be strengthened.

When you commit to completing this study guide, try to set apart a time, daily or weekly, to read through the lessons without distraction. Have your Bible nearby when you read the study guide, so you're ready to look up verses if you need to. If you want to use a notebook to write down your thoughts, be sure to have that handy as well. Take your time to think through and answer the questions. If you plan on reading the study guide with a small group, be sure to read ahead and be prepared to take part in the weekly discussions.

Leader's Guide

Thank you for your commitment to lead a group through *In Search of the Savior—The Gospel of Mark, Volume 2*. Being a leader has its own rewards. You may discover that your walk with the Lord deepens through this experience. Throughout the study guide, your group will explore new topics and review study questions that encourage thought-provoking group discussion.

The lessons in this study guide are suitable for Sunday school classes, small-group studies, elective Bible studies, or home Bible study groups. Each lesson is structured to provoke thought and help you grow in your knowledge and understanding of God. There are multiple components in this section that can help you structure your lessons and discussion time, so make sure you read and consider each one.

Before You Begin

Before you begin each meeting, make sure you and your group are well-versed with the content of the chapter. Every person should have his or her own study guide so they can follow along and write in the study guide if need be. When possible, the study guide should be used with the corresponding compact disc series. You may wish to assign the study guide lesson as homework prior to the meeting of the group and then use the meeting time to listen to the CD and discuss the lesson.

To ensure that everyone has a chance to participate in the discussion, the ideal size for a group is around eight to ten people. If there are more than ten people, try to break up the bigger group into smaller subgroups. Make sure the members are committed to participating each week, as this will help create stability and help you better prepare the structure of the meeting.

At the beginning of the study each week, start the session with a question to challenge group members to think about the issues you will be discussing. The members can answer briefly, but the goal is to have an idea in their mind as you go over the lesson. This allows the group members to become engaged and ready to interact with the group.

After reviewing the lesson, try to initiate a free-flowing discussion. Invite group members to bring questions and insights they may have discovered to the next meeting, especially if they were unsure of the meaning of some parts of the lesson. Be prepared to discuss how biblical truth applies to the world we live in today.

Weekly Preparation

As the group leader, here are a few things you can do to prepare for each meeting:

- Choose whether or not you will play the CD message during your small group session.

   If you decide to play the CD message from Dr. Jeremiah as part of the meeting, you will need to adjust the group time accordingly.

- Make sure you are thoroughly familiar with the material in the lesson.

   Make sure you understand the content of the lesson so you know how to structure group time and you are prepared to lead group discussion.

- Decide, ahead of time, which questions you plan to discuss.

   Depending on how much time you have each week, you may not be able to reflect on every question. Select specific questions which you feel will evoke the best discussion.

- Take prayer requests.

   At the end of your discussion, take prayer requests from your group members and pray for each other.

Structuring the Discussion Time

If you need help in organizing your time when planning your group Bible study, here are two schedules, for sixty minutes and ninety minutes, which can give you a structure for the lesson:

Option 1 (Listen to Audio CD)	60 Minutes	90 Minutes
Welcome: Members arrive and get settled.	N/A	5 minutes
Getting Started Question: Prepares the group for interacting with one another.	Welcome and Getting Started 5 minutes	15 minutes
Message: Listen to the audio CD.	40 minutes	40 minutes
Discussion: Discuss group study questions.	10 minutes	25 minutes
Prayer and Application: Final application for the week and prayer before dismissal.	5 minutes	5 minutes

Option 2 (No Audio CD)	60 Minutes	90 Minutes
Welcome: Members arrive and get settled.	5 minutes	10 minutes
Getting Started Question: Prepares the group for interacting with one another.	10 minutes	10 minutes
Message: Review the lesson.	15 minutes	25 minutes
Discussion: Discuss group study questions.	25 minutes	35 minutes
Prayer and Application: Final application for the week and prayer before dismissal.	5 minutes	10 minutes

As the group leader, it is up to you to keep track of the time and keep things moving along according to your schedule. If your group is having a good discussion, don't feel the need to stop and move on to the next question. Remember, the purpose is to pull together ideas, and share unique insights on the lesson. Make time each week to discuss how to apply these truths to living for Christ today.

The purpose of discussion is for everyone to participate, but don't be concerned if certain group members are more quiet—they may be internally reflecting on the questions and need time to process their ideas before they can share them.

Group Dynamics

Leading a group study can be a rewarding experience for you and your group members—but that doesn't mean there won't be challenges. Certain members may feel uncomfortable discussing topics that they consider very personal, and might be afraid of being called on. Some members might have disagreements on specific issues. To help prevent these scenarios, consider the following ground rules:

- If someone has a question that may seem off topic, suggest that it is discussed at another time, or ask the group if they are okay with addressing that topic.

- If someone asks a question you don't know the answer to, confess that you don't know and move on. If you feel comfortable, invite other group members to give their opinions, or share their comments based on personal experience.

- If you feel like a couple of people are talking much more than others, direct questions to people who may not have shared yet. You could even ask the more dominating members to help draw out the quiet ones.

- When there is a disagreement, encourage the group members to process the matter in love. Invite members from opposing sides to evaluate their opinions and consider the ideas of the other members. Lead the group through Scripture that addresses the topic, and look for common ground.

When issues arise, remind your group to think of Scripture: "Love one another" (John 13:34), "If it is possible, as much as depends on you, live peaceably with all men" (Romans 12:18), and "Be quick to listen, slow to speak and slow to become angry" (James 1:19, NIV).

For Continuing Study

For a complete listing of Dr. Jeremiah's materials for personal and group study call 1-800-947-1993, go online to www.DavidJeremiah.org, or write to Turning Point, P.O. Box 3838, San Diego, CA 92163.

Dr. Jeremiah's *Turning Point* program is currently heard or viewed around the world on radio, television, and the Internet in English. *Momento Decisivo*, the Spanish translation of Dr. Jeremiah's messages, can be heard on radio in every Spanish speaking country in the world. The television broadcast is also broadcast by satellite throughout the Middle East with Arabic subtitles.

Contact Turning Point for radio and television program times and stations in your area, or visit our website at www.DavidJeremiah.org/stationlocator.

In Search of the Savior—
The Gospel of Mark

Volume 2

INTRODUCTION

This study guide encompasses just five chapters of God's Word —from Mark 4 to Mark 8. But you would be hard pressed to find more of the mighty power of God compacted and displayed in a grander manner anywhere else in the Bible. If there was ever any doubt that Jesus was the Son of God, it was forever thwarted by His actions in these pages. He demonstrated the awesome power of God in a variety of ways in these short stories.

First of all, Jesus displayed His power over nature in this section of Mark. Not once, but twice, He calmed violent storms on the Sea of Galilee that were threatening the lives of His disciples. And when Jesus stopped a storm, there wasn't a gradual decline in the elements. It went from maelstrom to smooth waters and still air—in an instant! He created the world and showed His complete control of it in these mighty acts of authority.

Jesus also displayed His power over demons in these stories. In one instance, He freed a man who was literally possessed by thousands of demons. The miraculous transformation of that man led to such widespread fame of Jesus' deeds that one of the subsequent miracles Jesus performed in these chapters was for a man who came for healing—based on the testimony of the man with legion possession! Later on, Jesus remotely cast the demon out of the daughter of a Gentile woman.

In many instances, Jesus showed His power over disease and death. By just touching the hem of His robe, a woman was healed from an issue of blood that had plagued her for years. And when a sick little girl died before Jesus could reach her house, He simply brought her back from death. In a deeply moving and physical way, Jesus also healed a man who had lost his hearing and his ability to speak, showing compassion and understanding for the man's deficient condition.

One of Jesus' most famous miracles is found in these pages: the feeding of the five thousand. But Jesus didn't just feed a large crowd once, for just a few verses later, He feeds a different crowd of four thousand. He took mere earthly elements like bread and fish and showed His complete power over His creation by multiplying them in the most incredible manner. The same Man who could calm storms and walk on the water was One who was attentive to the physical needs of His followers. Only God could be like that.

And finally, Jesus displayed power over the religious traditions of the day. He destroyed the Pharisees' oral traditions that were held above the Word of God. He also destroyed the notion that the Gospel was only for the Jew, dramatically moving and acting in ways that showed salvation was also available to the Gentile.

The disciples were witnesses to these miraculous acts of authority and power. They spent each day with Jesus and saw Him perform countless deeds that no mortal man could ever accomplish. And yet, in light of all that they saw and all that they knew, they still did not get it! They were still unaware or unwilling to see that Jesus was the Messiah, that He was God walking in the flesh among them. That is why Jesus sadly said to them in Mark 8:21, "How is it you do not understand?"

May the same not be said of us! Let's be dedicated to be people of the Word, who not only hold the Bible as God's truth for our lives but also recognize and honor Jesus Christ as the Way, the Truth, and the Life.

THE PERFECT STORM

Mark 4:35-41

In this lesson we behold Jesus exercising His power and authority over a fierce storm.

OUTLINE

Everyone would prefer for the Christian life to be nothing but sunny days and smooth sailing. That is why we often panic when things go off-course and we can't control the chaotic circumstances of our lives. But sometimes God allows storms to occur in our lives to teach us valuable lessons—and to demonstrate His awesome power.

   I.   **The Probability of Storms in Our Lives**

   II.   **The Paradox of Storms in Our Lives**

  III.   **The Presence in the Storms of Our Lives**

  IV.   **The Peace in the Storms of Our Lives**

   V.   **The Purpose of Storms in Our Lives**

  VI.   **The Product of Storms in Our Lives**

 VII.   **The Promises for the Storms of Our Lives**
       A. God's Word Assures Us of a Safe Landing
       B. God's Word Alerts Us to Some Stormy Seas
       C. God's Word Announces That the Savior Is on Board
       D. God's Word Affirms to Us That the Ship Is in Good Hands

On October 23, 1991, Hurricane Grace began forming fifty miles south of Bermuda. It was subsequently joined with another storm, a "nor'easter," and together its intensity grew with powerful winds and nearly one hundred-foot waves that decimated the Eastern Seaboard, causing over 200 million dollars' worth of damage and the loss of thirteen lives. Six of those lost were the crew aboard the *Andrea Gail*, a sword-fishing boat that sank in the high waves. The storm was unnamed for a while, but was eventually called "The Perfect Storm" because of the events that merged together with such devastating effect. That boat later became the focus of a book and a major motion picture entitled *The Perfect Storm*.

The term *perfect storm* refers to a series of events that individually are not powerful by themselves, but when they occur simultaneously, their power is increased exponentially. But perfect storms are not confined to just the physical world in which we live; we can have perfect storms in our own personal lives as well. These storms can involve mixtures of personal, relational, emotional, financial, and spiritual things. When they all come together, we can feel overwhelmed in our own perfect storm.

In the fourth chapter of Mark, there is a story featuring a perfect storm that involved Jesus and His disciples. The takeaway from this account will speak to all of us in one way or another, because no matter who you are, you have experienced some stormy weather in your individual life.

THE PROBABILITY OF STORMS IN OUR LIVES

Verse 37 tells us, "And a great windstorm arose, and the waves beat into the boat, so that it was already filling." This story about Jesus and the disciples on the Sea of Galilee is a reminder to all of us that there is a strong probability of storms in our lives. Just like no man is exempt from death, no man is exempt from the storms of life.

Here is the context for the story: It is evening, at the end of a very long and exhausting day. After the teaching of many parables, it was the decision of Jesus to leave Capernaum and go to the other side of the Sea of Galilee so that they could all get away from the crowd. The text says that the disciples took Jesus, "as He was," in the boat (Mark 4:36).

The Bible says that when they left Capernaum to sail to the other side, a flotilla of boats went with them. They had not gone very far when a fierce storm arose. It is important to understand that the Sea of Galilee is seven hundred feet below sea level, but it is surrounded by mountains, one of which (Mount Hermon) is more than nine thousand feet above sea level. When the cold air from the mountains meets the warm air from the floor of the desert, storms can descend upon the Sea of Galilee quickly and with great severity.

The great windstorm that arose on this particular day could be described as a "furious squall." Mark's account uses a Greek word to describe the storm that is best translated as the word *hurricane*. Matthew describes it using a different word: *seismos*—from which we get our word *earthquake*. The storm that day was like there had been an earthquake in the middle of the Sea of Galilee, and it came upon the disciples suddenly. If you visit Israel even today, the Galilean fishermen describe these still-occurring kinds of storms as "shark storms."

Well, the storm on this day was so violent that the waves were breaking over the boat and filling it with water. And while the boat was filling up with water, the hearts of the disciples were filling up with fear. And I am sure that the same could be said of all of us— that when we experience a storm, we, too, fill up with fear.

THE PARADOX OF STORMS IN OUR LIVES

There is a paradox that could escape us if we do not think deeply about what is going on here. The disciples who were in this storm with Jesus were in God's perfect will, yet they ended up in God's perfect storm. It was Jesus who said, "Let us cross over to the other side." The disciples were simply following His instructions. They were assisting Him in His ministry and were following Him, helping Him preach the Gospel. And yet, these men found themselves terrified in the midst of a storm, tossed to and fro, in danger of drowning, with fear overtaking their hearts.

Here's another way to look at it: The disciples were not in the storm because they were disobedient—they were in the storm because they were obedient. They were not in the storm because they were doing something wrong; they were in the storm because they were doing something right! Don't let anyone ever tell you that if you're going through a storm in your life, it is because you have done something wrong. It well may be, but it is not necessarily so. Storms come to all of us no matter who we are, and oftentimes it has nothing to do with what you've been doing, but everything to do with what God wants to accomplish in your life.

The Presence in the Storms of Our Lives

Notice that in verse 38, there is a presence in the storm. "But He was in the stern, asleep on a pillow. And they awoke Him and said to Him, 'Teacher, do You not care that we are perishing?'" Jesus was present during the storm. The disciples were trying to get Jesus away from the crowd so that He could recover His strength. And as they headed to the other shore, Jesus was so fatigued from many hours of teaching that He was sleeping against a cushion in the stern of the boat. By the way, this is the only time in the Bible where we are told that Jesus slept, and it was in the middle of a storm.

In just a moment, Jesus will be awakened. And in that moment, He will still the storm in an extraordinary exhibition of power. But before that He awakes, His weary body is resting. This display of weakness and omnipotence is not in conflict but is a perfect picture of the two natures of our Lord as He walked upon this earth.[1]

In His humanity, He was weary; in His divinity, He stilled the storms. He was the Son of God and the Son of Man, perfectly, in one person. And in just this little vignette, we see both sides of Jesus at the same time.

The Peace in the Storms of Our Lives

The Bible says in verse 39 that Jesus "arose and rebuked the wind, and said to the sea, 'Peace, be still!' And the wind ceased and there was a great calm." This truly was a miracle! With just His voice, the Lord Jesus rebuked the wind. The word *rebuked* used here is the same word that is used for rebuking a demon. Jesus rebuked the wind just like it was a demon.

And when He said to the sea, "Peace, be still," the word used there in the language of the New Testament translates as, "Be muzzled." Jesus was saying to the waves, "Stop it! Be quiet!"

In essence, there were two miracles: The miracle of the wind was accompanied by the miracle of the waves. You may say, "Wasn't that just the same miracle?" No! You could possibly misunderstand the miracle of the wind, but there is no misunderstanding the miracle of the waves.

If you live on a coast you know that after storms are over, the waves still beat against the shoreline for hours after the storm has ceased. It takes a long time for the effects of the storm to cease. But on this particular day, when Jesus turned to the waves and said, "Be still," in a moment, the water was like glass that you could see your reflection in.

But wait a minute. There is a third miracle that we haven't yet uncovered. Jesus stilled the wind and He calmed the waves, but now He must deal with the disciples. And some people believe that was a greater miracle than either of the first two—getting the agitated disciples to reclaim their composure after their difficult experience during the storm.

THE PURPOSE OF STORMS IN OUR LIVES

The question then looms: Why did this storm happen? Jesus obviously allowed the storm to happen, for He was in the boat. He was in control; it was His will that it happened. And He allowed it so that His disciples might learn to trust Him. Through storms, our Lord teaches us many lessons, doesn't He? When the wind and waves are raging He reminds us of our own human frailness and our own total dependence upon Him to live.

The psalmist David understood this. Here are his words from Psalm 119:

Before I was afflicted I went astray,
But now I keep Your word. (verse 67)
It is good for me that I have been afflicted,
That I may learn Your statutes. (verse 71)
I know, O Lord, that Your judgments are right,
And that in faithfulness You have afflicted me. (verse 75)

Sometimes when you get into a storm, God is trying to do a mid-course correction on your life. You may think you are going in the right direction doing your own thing, so God will send a storm to say, "Wait a minute, you are going in the wrong direction. You need to go this way."

When you go through a storm as a believer, just know that God is up to something. He never lets you experience anything that is not for your good. He has a plan. And if you will respond to Him in faith and not in fear, God will show you what He is up to. He will take you to the other side.

THE PRODUCT OF STORMS IN OUR LIVES

What does a storm produce? In Mark 4:40-41 we read, "But He said to them, 'Why are you so fearful? How is it that you have no faith?' And they feared exceedingly, and said to one another, 'Who can this be, that even the wind and the sea obey Him!'"

Following the miracle of stilling the storm, this question by the disciples is significant. The disciples were more afraid after the storm died down than they were when the storm was raging. When they were in the storm and they didn't know what to do, the Bible says they were fearful. When they saw Jesus overcome the storm with only the sound of His voice, the Bible says they were *very* fearful. They became terrified at the power He displayed over the wind and sea.

This is a confusing situation. While they're in the midst of the storm, the disciples can see the storm and they are trying to handle it. But when Jesus stills the storm, they're totally at a loss! So Jesus rebuked the wind, He rebuked the waves, and then He had to rebuke the disciples, chiding them for having no faith.

So perhaps today you are full of fear. Maybe your fear is just fear in general. Your fear may stem from some unspoken problem that does not seem to have any apparent solution. This is an important truth I want you to learn from this lesson—it is through the storms and afflictions and hardships of life that you will grow in your faith. Without them, you will be captive to the terrible tyranny of self. The Lord Jesus wants to help you grow and develop your spiritual muscles through your storms. Storms produce faith.

THE PROMISES FOR THE STORMS OF OUR LIVES

It is not always God's purpose to immediately relieve all pain from our lives—sometimes He uses that pain to help us become the people we could not be without it. But there are clear promises for the storms of our lives that we can be assured of at all times.

God's Word Assures Us of a Safe Landing

Before the storm ever happened, Jesus said to the disciples in Mark 4:35, "Let us cross over to the other side." A few verses later in Mark 5:1, we read, "Then they came to the other side of the sea." When Jesus says you're going to the other side, you will reach the other side!

The storm was an incidental thing in terms of the ultimate journey. If the disciples had just understood that Jesus intended to reach the other side, they would have settled down and taken confidence in the ultimate destination.

And we can apply that same lesson to our lives as Christians. This world is not our home—we are temporary dwellers—we are just passing through. Our ultimate destination is heaven. Since we know that we will reach the other side, it gives perspective to the storms we encounter along the way. We might be having a stormy journey, but God's Word assures us of a safe landing.

God's Word Alerts Us to Some Stormy Seas

Secondly, God's Word alerts us that, between here and there, there will be some heavy storms we will face. This is a fact that Christians really need to be aware of. The Bible does not say that when you become saved, you will never have any storms. Exactly the opposite is true!

Second Timothy 3:12 says that "all who desire to live godly in Christ Jesus will suffer persecution." The Bible teaches us that there are storms out there that we will no doubt have to face in our earthly lives.

God's Word Announces That the Savior Is on Board

We need to remember that safety is not the absence of a storm —safety is the presence of the Savior. Sometimes Jesus does not chase the storm away, but He does not leave us to face it alone—He remains with us through the storm. And the presence of Jesus alone is enough to sustain us during any storm we encounter.

God's Word Affirms to Us That the Ship Is in Good Hands

Who's in charge? From the calm before the storm, through the darkest and roughest hour of the wind and waves, to the rolling away of the dark clouds, Jesus was there—and He was in control. It may not have seemed like that to the disciples, but we know that Jesus was in total control because when He spoke, everyone saw what happened.

So it all boils down to this question: Is Jesus in your boat? If you are facing a storm or are in one now, make sure that Jesus is in your boat—or better yet, that you are in His boat. If you are, you can be assured that you will reach your final destination no matter how dire the circumstances seem, because the Lord of the wind and waves is traveling beside you.

Note

1. R. Kent Hughes, *Mark, Volume 1: Jesus, Servant and Savior* (Wheaton, IL: Crossway Books, 1989), 114.

1. Read Mark 4:35-38.

   a. Who suggested that Jesus and His disciples sail to the other side? (verse 35) Why is this such a crucial detail to this story?

   b. What unique fact does verse 36 give us? Why might that be important to the story?

   c. What was the biggest danger for those aboard the boat that night? (verse 37)

   d. Where was Jesus during the storm? What was He doing? (verse 38)

   e. What did the disciples accuse Jesus of upon waking Him? (verse 38) Why was this such a ridiculous accusation for them to assert?

2. Read Mark 4:39-41.

   a. What was the first thing Jesus did to stop the storm? (verse 39)

   b. What did He then say to the sea? What was the result?

   c. Explain why it makes sense that Jesus stopped the wind before He calmed the waves.

   d. In response to their accusation from verse 38, what did Jesus accuse the disciples of in verse 40?

   e. What was their emotional response to Jesus' words and His calming of the sea?

   f. In spite of all that had happened, what were the disciples unable to realize after this miracle?

GROUP QUESTIONS

1. Read Psalm 46.

   a. List all of the earthly, physical, and manmade elements that we should not fear because of the refuge and strength of our God.

   b. How does verse 10 contrast with all the other images and actions in this Psalm?

   c. Discuss why the psalmist chose to repeat verses 7 and 11. Why is that phrase critical to understanding this Psalm?

2. Read Psalm 93.

   a. One of the great phrases of this Psalm is that the earth "cannot be moved." Why will the world not be moved? List and discuss the reasons why found in this Psalm.

b. What three actions are caused by the floods in this Psalm? (verse 3)

c. In response to the actions of the floods, what is God mightier than? (verse 3)

d. Do you think Jesus knew this Psalm and perhaps even had it in mind when He performed this miracle? Discuss as a group why or why not.

3. Read Psalm 107:23-32.

a. Those who sail on the sea get to experience and realize what two things? (verse 24)

b. Read aloud Mark 4:35-41, then read aloud Psalm 107:23-32. Discuss and list the similarities between the Gospel story and the words of this Psalm.

c. Why is it important for us to realize that God is greater than any physical storm the earth can produce?

DID YOU KNOW?

In the book of Mark there is another episode that takes place in a storm on the Sea of Galilee. This is when Jesus walked on the water toward the disciples (Mark 6:45-52), who were once again struggling on a boat in the water. What is often missed in the setting of this story is that this event also occurred during a violent storm! Jesus was not walking on placid waters, but on rough, wind-hewn waves. It makes this miracle even more amazing! It is also interesting to note that in both of these stories, Jesus had to reprimand the disciples for their lack of faith. Sometimes we learn the lesson the hard way—often more than once!

LEGION

Mark 5:1-20

In this lesson we watch as Jesus casts out demons from a horribly possessed man.

OUTLINE

In His time on the earth, Jesus performed many varieties of miracles. He healed the sick, He changed the weather, and He even revealed His power by multiplying bread and fish and changing water into wine. But one of His most dramatic and powerful displays of authority is when He cast out demons from a man who suffered from possession.

I. **The Work of Satan in the World**
    A. The Reality of Demon Possession
    B. The Result of Demon Possession

II. **The Work of Society in the World**
    A. Society Could Not Control the Man
    B. Society Could Not Cure the Man

III. **The Work of the Savior in the World**
    A. Jesus Arranged His Encounter With This Man
    B. Jesus Acknowledged Worship by This Man
    C. Jesus Assaulted the Demons in This Man
    D. Jesus Allowed the Demons to Enter Into the Swine
    E. Jesus Answered the Questions About This Man
    F. Jesus Assigned a Mission to This Man

After Jesus calmed the storm on the Sea of Galilee, He and His disciples "came to the other side of the sea, to the country of the Gadarenes" (Mark 5:1). Also known as Gadara, this location was on the eastern shore of the Sea of Galilee, with the city itself just six miles inland from the lake.

A short distance south of the city was a spot where an area of steep hills came right down and emptied into the water. In that area were many graves where the people of that area had buried their dead in tombs carved out of the limestone rock. This was essentially a cemetery of that time.

The importance of the story we are going to study here is seen in the fact that Jesus is going to perform a miracle in Gentile country. Gadara is a Gentile town. This is not about a Jewish country or Jewish culture, for nothing about this story is kosher. Everything about it is unclean; the spirits are unclean, the tombs are unclean, and the pigs are unclean.

In this alien place, Jesus is going to prove that His authority is just as great in a Gentile culture as it is in a Jewish culture. Jesus is Lord for, and of, all people.

This story shows us three things: what Satan can do in the world, what society can do in the world, and what the Savior can do in the world.

THE WORK OF SATAN IN THE WORLD

Let's look first at the evidence that Satan really does exist and has an effect on the world.

The Reality of Demon Possession

In Mark 5:2 we read that "when He had come out of the boat, immediately there met Him out of the tombs a man with an unclean spirit." As one writer put it, "Jesus came straight from His confrontation with the storm in nature to confront an equally violent storm in human nature."[1]

Matthew, Mark, and Luke all tell this story, but Mark is particularly detailed about this man who was one of the demon-possessed people living in that area. He focused his whole attention on this one very outwardly and demonstratively demon-possessed man.

The Bible tells us that this man who met Jesus when He beached His boat in Gadara was a man who was filled with an "unclean spirit."

We are not told how this evil spirit possessed him, but we do know that unclean spirits can take hold of a person when that person willingly cultivates the dark side of evil. This is serious stuff. The reality of demonic activity is real today.

The Result of Demon Possession

The next three verses tell us about this man and the suffering he endured because of his possession: He "had his dwelling among the tombs; and no one could bind him, not even with chains, because he had often been bound with shackles and chains. And he had pulled the chains apart, and the shackles broken in pieces; neither could anyone tame him. And always, night and day, he was in the mountains and in the tombs, crying out and cutting himself with stones" (Mark 5:3-5).

This man was not criminally insane, nor was he merely under the influence of passion and rage. This man was Satan's poster child. He was possessed not by just one demon but by so many demons that he called himself "Legion."

The description of this man is one of the saddest stories of human wretchedness in the Bible. He was so violent that he was treated not as a human being but as a wild animal.

Scripture says that no man could tame him.

THE WORK OF SOCIETY IN THE WORLD

Next, let's take a look at how society failed to save this poor, wretched man.

Society Could Not Control the Man

Verse 4 demonstrates that society could not control this man because every time they put him in chains and handcuffs, he broke free of them. Society had probably driven this man into the wilderness to live among the tombs because of his wild demonstrations of his possession. Whenever they had tried to restrain him, the demons were so many and so strong that whatever restraints they put in place were immediately broken. They couldn't control him. This was an impossible case!

Society Could Not Cure the Man

Many times, society thinks they have the cure for sin by calling it something else. In verse 5 we learn we see the symptoms of Legion's possession, that "always, night and day, he was in the mountains and in the tombs, crying out and cutting himself with stones."

This poor demented man could be heard by the people nearby as he cried out from the tombs throughout the day and night.

As he cried in his wretchedness, we are told that he was taking sharp stones and cutting his body. Did you think that the modern practice of "cutting" by many troubled young people is something new? It has been going on for a long time. He was destroying his body and the community he lived in was helpless to cure him of these symptoms.

The society of that day was not equipped to deal with this man. And after all these years of study and experimentation, we are no better equipped to deal with his affliction than they were. Today we would try to medicate him to wellness. If everything else failed, we would institutionalize him.

But this man was not insane. He wasn't suffering from a chemical imbalance. And he wasn't schizophrenic or delusional. He was demon-possessed! And only meeting Jesus Christ could heal him then or now. Jesus really is the only answer.

THE WORK OF THE SAVIOR IN THE WORLD

Now that we have established what Satan does and how society fails when attempting to deal with it, let's look at how Jesus intervened as we walk step-by-step through this story as Jesus encountered this problem.

Jesus Arranged His Encounter With This Man

This was not a random happening, for Jesus arranged this encounter with this man. Jesus particularly came to Gadara for one reason, and that was to confront this man. He came, He did what He came to do, and the Bible says when that was accomplished, He got back into the boat and left.

Did you know that Jesus never does anything by chance? Jesus went through a raging storm to arrive at the place just where this demon-possessed man would be. Some have suggested that the storm might have been Satan's attempt to keep Jesus from coming to this man's rescue. Maybe Satan thought he could drown the Savior before He came and confronted his poster boy for demon possession. Nevertheless, Jesus successfully arranged the encounter with this man.

Jesus Acknowledged Worship by This Man

What happens next in verse 6 is startling and amazing: "When he saw Jesus from afar, he ran and worshiped Him." It is hard to imagine what this man looked like when Jesus first saw him. He was no doubt covered with wounds and scabs and scars and fresh blood.

He stood in front of Jesus—this naked, pitiful creature—he shrieked, and then he spoke, saying: "What have I to do with you, Jesus, Son of the Most High God?" (verse 7)

Did you know that the demons know more about Jesus than a lot of people that go to church? James 2:19 says, "You believe that there is one God. You do well. Even the demons believe—and tremble!"

The demons in this man not only believed that Jesus was the Son of God but they also believed in hell. They believed that one day they would be cast into hell and tormented, and they were asking the Lord Jesus not to do it now. Luke 8:31 says that "they begged Him that He would not command them to go out into the abyss."

Believing in the deity of Christ and in hell is more than many religious people believe today, including some so-called preachers of recent vintage. Yet this is one of the most pitiful sights in all of the world, for here is a person whose mind is so torn that he worships while he is cursing and confesses while he is blaspheming. If ever a picture of Satan's ultimate motive is seen, here it is.[2]

Jesus Assaulted the Demons in This Man

As this man came up to Jesus screaming his words, Jesus looked at him and this is what happened: "For He said to him, 'Come out of the man, unclean spirit!' Then He asked him, 'What is your name?' And he answered, saying, 'My name is Legion; for we are many'" (Mark 5:8-9).

When Jesus spoke, the demons that were controlling this man knew that Jesus had power over them. They knew that they did not have the right to this man's body. They had laughed at the feeble attempts of the inhabitants of Gadara to control them, but Jesus was no laughing matter. And when Jesus asked, "What is your name?" a demon answered the Lord's question and expressed the horror of this man's situation. He was possessed by a "legion" of demons.

A Roman legion could consist of as many as six thousand men. That's what a legion normally was. Think of being possessed with one demon, and then try to wrap your arms around the idea of being possessed with six thousand demons, all of which are determined to destroy you and everybody around you. It is difficult to comprehend, but when Jesus said, "Come out now," immediately the man was set free.

Jesus Allowed the Demons to Enter Into the Swine

The next part of the story is very intriguing. The demons are now disembodied, but they don't have a host. They are out there in no man's land. And the Bible says that they asked permission of Jesus to enter a herd of swine.

Notice that Jesus didn't assign them to the swine—He just gave them permission. Why would He do that? Only to make this point: that Jesus has the ability to destroy the demons in human beings, and then display what they do to anyone they possess. This is a lesson well learned.

What did they do when they went into the swine? They ran down the steep hill and into the water, and all of the swine drowned. Once they swine drowned, the only thing left was this one man who had been cleansed of evil.

Jesus Answered the Questions About This Man

In verse 14 we read, "So those who fed the swine fled, and they told it in the city and in the country. And they went out to see what it was that had happened." The swine herders didn't own these pigs; they were just the shepherds who were managing them. They were the swine herders, not the swine owners. The swine owners were living in Gadara, so they ran and told them what happened to their stock.

When they got to the place where this happened, the first thing they all saw were all the dead carcasses of the swine littering the shore of the sea. Enough time had now passed that they would have washed up on the shore. And when they came to Jesus and the saw the one "who had been demon-possessed and had the legion, sitting and clothed and in his right mind," then they were afraid. So in verse 17, "they began to plead with Him to depart from their region."

This is an amazing request. Here's a man who has handled the number-one social problem troubling the community for some time, totally transforming the derelict who haunted them day and night with his cries. Then, the city leaders walk back into that situation and say to the Healer, "Leave us—and don't ever come back!"

Welcome to the confrontation between spirituality and materialism. When Jesus healed the man, He also destroyed the business of the swine herders. They were absolutely infuriated that Jesus had destroyed their means of wealth, and they didn't care anything about this poor man who had been healed and transformed.

Jesus Assigned a Mission to This Man

The Bible says that when Jesus was finished with the legion of Gadara, His work was finished, so He got back into the boat to leave. Verse 18 tells us, "And when He got into the boat, he who had been demon-possessed begged Him that he might be with Him."

Can you imagine how grateful this man was? All his adult life, forces over which he had no control had controlled him. He would have been a tortured outcast for all his days, but then Jesus came and made him whole.

This man was transformed, and he now saw a future life that he never dreamed could ever be possible for one such as him. And he loved Jesus. He had been forgiven much and he loved much. And he wasn't about to let Jesus get out of his sight if he could help it.

Verse 19 says, "However, Jesus did not permit him, but said to him, 'Go home to your friends, and tell them what great things the Lord has done for you, and how He has had compassion on you.'" Jesus had a higher priority for this man; in essence he was the first missionary to the Gentiles because when he went home, he began to tell everybody in Gentile Gadara what Jesus had done for him.

But this man wasn't satisfied to just go home and tell his friends. Verse 20 says, "And he departed and began to proclaim in Decapolis all that Jesus had done for him; and all marveled." *Decapolis* is a word that means "ten cities." So Gadara was a part of a ten-city coalition. And when this man told his family about what Jesus had done, that simply wasn't enough.

So this transformed man did not limit his testimony to his hometown. He told everybody! And once you begin to find the thrill of sharing your witness, you, too, won't be satisfied just to share it with a few people. You'll have to spread your territory out, and tell everyone how Jesus changed your life!

Notes

1. R. Kent Hughes, *Mark, Volume 1: Jesus, Servant and Savior* (Wheaton, IL: Crossway Books, 1989), 118.

2. David L. McKenna, *The Preacher's Commentary—Mark* (Nashville, TN: Thomas Nelson), 109.

PERSONAL QUESTIONS

1. Read Mark 5:1-10.

   a. How much time did Jesus and the disciples have on the shore before they encountered the troubled man? (verse 2)

   b. Where did this man come out of to meet Jesus? (verse 2) Why do you think he chose to live there?

   c. How had the people of the area sought to tame and bind this man? What had been the result? (verses 3-4)

   d. What two things did this man do both night and day? Where did he stay most of the time? (verse 5)

   e. At just a glimpse of Jesus, what two things did the possessed man do? (verse 6)

f. What did this man implore Jesus not to do? (verse 7)

g. What incredible questions did Jesus ask of the unclean spirit? What was the answer? (verse 9)

h. What curious request was made by the unclean spirits to Jesus? (verse 10)

2. Read Mark 5:11-20.

a. Where did the demons ask Jesus to send them? (verse 11)

b. How many were there? What was the result of that action? (verse 13)

c. Who were the first witnesses of this miracle to share it with the outside world? (verse 14)

d. When everyone returned to the scene, what did they see? (verse 15)

e. At seeing the once-possessed man in his right mind, what was their emotional reaction? (verse 15)

f. How did they respond to Jesus in light of this miracle? (verse 17)

g. What did the once-possessed man want to do? What did Jesus tell him to do instead? (verses 18-19)

h. What was the community response to that man's testimony? (verse 20)

GROUP QUESTIONS

1. Read Ephesians 6:10-17. Discuss the following questions.

   a. Paul tells us as believers to be strong in what two ways? (verse 10)

   b. Why are we to wear the whole armor of God? What does the armor of God protect us against? (verse 11)

   c. Verse 12 says that we don't wrestle against physical things, but against what four forces? List and discuss them and how they played a role in this lesson.

   d. The armor of God is provided so that we can do what two things? (verse 13)

e. List the different parts of the armor of God that are described in verses 14-18. Which of these are you most successful at wearing? Which do you struggle to display? Discuss and explain why.

2. Read Mark 5:6-7, 13.

   a. The possessed man "ran and worshiped" Jesus when he saw Him. What does this say about Jesus' place in the universe? Would we react in the same way? Do we?

   b. Verse 13 says Jesus gave the demons "permission" to enter the swine. What does the word *permission* entail in this situation and explain about the power and place of Jesus?

DID YOU KNOW?

You can visit the location of this miracle even today in Israel. The place is now called Kursi, and it is found on the east bank of the Sea of Galilee near the Golan Heights. Although this location now bears the remnants of a monastery dating to the Byzantine era, this significant site had been forgotten for more than 1,300 years until it was rediscovered during the 1976 Six Day War, when construction of a road revealed an archaeological treasure trove. And in 1980, a small chapel was found that contained access to a cave—very possibly the cave where that tortured man first met Jesus and was freed from his demonic possession once and for all.

JESUS' POWER OVER DISEASE AND DEATH

Mark 5:21-43

In this lesson we see Jesus change the lives of two very different people on one special day.

OUTLINE

Jesus performed countless miracles in His time on the earth. But some miracles stand out over others. These two miracles described in the book of Mark are remarkable because they offer such a stark contrast in personalities and backgrounds. On a certain day in a certain place, Jesus totally changed the lives of two quite dissimilar people.

I. **A Divine Introduction**
    A. The Ruler Who Came to Jesus
    B. The Respect He Had for Jesus
    C. The Request He Made of Jesus
    D. The Response He Got From Jesus

II. **A Divine Intrusion**
    A. The Woman Who Came for Healing
    B. The Way Jesus Healed Her

III. **A Divine Intervention**
    A. The Discouraging Message
    B. The Defining Ministry
    C. The Dreaded March
    D. The Despairing Mourners
    E. The Dynamic Miracle

After Jesus' miracle involving Legion and the swine, He returned to Capernaum—where He is about to perform two more miracles. These miracles are especially interesting because they are wrought on two people from two totally different backgrounds. And their stories are woven together by Mark in a marvelous way that will catch your attention.

Here we meet two people of desperate representations. One of them is rich; the other is poor. One is accepted; the other is an outcast. One is in a family; the other is by himself. Both individuals are beyond human help, and their adversity binds their souls together and allows them to be recipients of God's incredible power in a short span of time.[1]

Mark's presentation of this story is both interesting and easy to follow. The story starts with a divine introduction, stops for a divine intrusion, and ends with a divine intervention.

A DIVINE INTRODUCTION

Let's begin this lesson with the divine introduction. The Bible tells us in verse 22 that a ruler came to Jesus—his name was Jairus.

The Ruler Who Came to Jesus

Jesus once again is traveling by boat and when he arrives to the other side of the sea, a ruler came to Jesus: "And behold, one of the rulers of the synagogue came, Jairus by name." Amid the great crowd that gathered to welcome Jesus back to Capernaum was a very important man who made his way through the crowd to where Jesus was.

Jairus was a ruler of the synagogue. The synagogues of that day were ruled by a group of elders. Jairus well may have been the number-one elder in the Capernaum synagogue. As a man of great importance, there is no doubt that everyone in that crowd gathered at the shore knew him. If you knew Capernaum, you knew Jairus.

The Respect He Had for Jesus

The remarkable thing about this meeting is "when he saw Him, he fell at His feet" (Mark 5:22). When we first see this, we might think he is worshiping the Lord Jesus; but if you study it carefully, you will realize that he fell at His feet in desperation. He fell at His feet with the absolute certainty that if Jesus didn't help him in his situation, there was no hope.

Jairus acknowledged that only Jesus had the power to do what this man required. And so, he came out of desperation and cast himself at the feet of Jesus.

The Request He Made of Jesus

In verse 23 we discover that Jairus' situation is desperate: "My little daughter lies at the point of death. Come and lay Your hands on her, that she may be healed, and she will live." All of us who have had children or have grandchildren have no trouble understanding the emotion of this moment. Children are so helpless when they are small, and nothing is so helpless as a little child who is ill.

Luke 8:42 informs us that this little girl was his only child and he loved his little daughter like he loved life. She had gotten sick and had gotten worse, and the Bible tells us in the book of Luke that she was about to die.

In verse 42 of this text, we are told that she was twelve years old. And since we know that Jesus spent a lot of time in Capernaum, it's evident that Jesus knew who this little girl was. She was the preacher's kid, so to speak. And if you're the preacher's kid, you hang out at the church all the time.

So, whenever Jesus came there to teach, He would have known who she was. And it's probable that she knew who Jesus was. And now this little girl, the daughter of the ruler of the synagogue, was lying in her bed at home, about to die.

The Response He Got From Jesus

We learn in verse 24 that "Jesus went with him, and a great multitude followed Him and thronged Him." Jesus was always being thronged. When Jesus began walking toward Jairus' home, He didn't go alone—everyone was following Him.

These weren't necessarily people who followed Him out of faith; they followed Him out of curiosity. They had heard all the things that He did. And so, when He headed out toward Jairus' home, He had a whole crowd with Him.

A DIVINE INTRUSION

On the way to Jairus' house, there is a divine intrusion.

The Woman Who Came for Healing

In verse 25, we read that someone came to Jesus on His way to Jairus' house and interrupted the journey. It was a woman who had come for healing.

1. How Desperate She Was

Note the desperation of her circumstances in verses 25 and 26: "Now a certain woman had a flow of blood for twelve years, and had suffered many things from many physicians. She had spent all that she had and was no better, but rather grew worse."

There is about to be an intrusion in Jesus' journey to Jairus' house, an intrusion that you could well imagine was very disconcerting to Jairus. Yet the woman who intruded was just as desperate as Jairus was! She had a problem that was just as dire as the problem of Jairus' little girl. She had tried for years to be healed and she couldn't be helped.

Please take special notice that in this text the description, "twelve years" is found twice. Jairus' little girl was twelve years old—and the woman had been sick for twelve years. So while Jairus had been enjoying his daughter for twelve years, this woman had been enduring pain and sickness and despair for that same amount of time.

The sickness that she had was, under Jewish law, a defilement that made her an outcast—untouchable by anyone. This woman had suffered pain and embarrassment. Like Jairus, she turned to Jesus as her last hope. If Jesus couldn't help her, she would live out her life as a broken woman.

2. How Determined She Was

She was not only desperate, she was determined: "When she heard about Jesus, she came behind Him in the crowd and touched His garment. For she said, 'If only I may touch His clothes, I shall be made well'" (Mark 5:27-28).

When this woman heard about Jesus, she found out where He was. And even though He was on His way to help Jairus' daughter amidst a huge throng of people, she wasn't going to allow that crowd to prevent her from reaching Him. She moved in amidst the crowd and she worked her way up to where Jesus was.

When she got close enough, she reached out and grabbed hold of His clothing. She had such faith to believe that even if she didn't receive Jesus' full attention, if she could just touch His robe, she would be healed.

The Way Jesus Healed Her

There are three characteristics to note about how Jesus healed this woman.

1. He Healed Her Immediately

In verse 29 we discover that her healing was instantaneous: "Immediately the fountain of her blood was dried up, and she felt in her body that she was healed of the affliction." She was not disappointed. What she had hoped and believed would happen did indeed take place.

As soon as she touched Jesus, she was healed with the very same power that had quieted the wind and the waves, with the same power that rebuked the demons. With that very same power He healed this woman of her sickness, and He did it without even mentioning it or having it become a public matter.

2. He Healed Her Inconspicuously

Notice what happened next: "And Jesus, immediately knowing in Himself that power had gone out of Him, turned around in the crowd and said, 'Who touched My clothes?' But His disciples said to Him, 'You see the multitude thronging You, and You say, "Who touched Me?"'" (Mark 5:30-31)

Jesus was surrounded by people. He was being pushed by people. He was being touched on every side. But Jesus knew that He had been touched by a touch of faith.

This woman believed so much that if she could just touch Jesus' clothes, she would be healed. She followed through on what she believed, acted to find where Jesus was, and reached out to touch Him. It was done so inconspicuously that when she did touch Him and Jesus turned around and said, "Who touched Me?" the disciples were totally perplexed, because Jesus was being touched every which way by the crowds around Him.

But you see, Jesus wanted this woman to know that He knew who she was. Jesus wanted her to know that she was not healed because she was aggressive enough to touch Him—she was healed because He wanted her to be healed. And He wanted her to know that He knew who she was and that she was healed by His power and not merely by her own action.

3. He Healed Her Intentionally

The healing was purposeful and intentional, for in verses 33 and 34 we learn, "But the woman, fearing and trembling, knowing what had happened to her, came and fell down before Him and told Him the whole truth. And He said to her, 'Daughter, your faith has made you well. Go in peace, and be healed of your affliction.'"

The question is: Was she healed because Jesus healed her, or was she healed because of her faith?[2]

The answer is yes. She was healed because of her faith to come to Jesus, but her ultimate healing was at the will of the Lord Jesus Christ. It was His power that healed her. Faith was the door that opened her to the power of Jesus, but Jesus did the ultimate work. He healed her and then He referred to her as "daughter," which is the only time in the Bible Jesus ever called anybody by that name.

And then there is poor Jairus. He is just standing there watching this. His daughter is dying and he wants Jesus to get to his daughter, but Jesus stops along the way to deal with this woman. And Jairus is about to get some news that will change everything about what he has come to Jesus for.

A Divine Intervention

This divine introduction and divine intrusion are now going to be fulfilled in a divine intervention. The Lord Jesus is going to intervene in the life of this family.

The Discouraging Message

But first there is a discouraging message. Verse 35 says that "while He was still speaking, some came from the ruler of the synagogue's house who said, 'Your daughter is dead. Why trouble the Teacher any further?'"

Messengers from Jairus' home had come to find him and tell him he didn't need to go on his journey to find the Teacher anymore, for what they had feared would happen had indeed happened. His little girl had died.

The way the story is told in the text makes it evident they didn't believe Jesus could have done anything at that point anyway. They don't call Him "Jesus." They call Him the "Teacher." They thought there was nothing Jesus could do about it now.

It is not hard to imagine the thoughts that ran through Jairus' mind. He was thinking, *Lord Jesus, if You hadn't stopped to help this woman, my little girl might still be available to be healed.* What emotions Jairus must have felt at that moment.

The Defining Ministry

As soon as Jesus heard the bad news that had come from Jairus' house, He didn't waste a minute trying to encourage Jarius' heart. Upon hearing the news, Jesus said, "Do not be afraid; only believe" (verse 36). This was not a time for fear; this was a time for faith.

The Dreaded March

At that point Jesus turned to the crowd that was thronging Him and said, "You can't go any further. I'm taking my three most disciples with Me—James, John, and Peter—and the three of us will go to Jairus' house and see his daughter." Jesus didn't want to turn the sorrow of this family into some sort of bizarre spectacle. He wanted to deal with the sorrow of this family like anyone would—in quietness and privacy and dignity. But they still had to march to the house.

The Despairing Mourners

When they finally got to the house, something was already going on there. There was "a tumult and those who wept and wailed loudly. When He came in, He said to them, 'Why make this commotion and weep? The child is not dead, but sleeping'" (Mark 5:38-39).

Please note that Jesus wasn't scolding the family members for their sorrow. In Palestine in those days, when someone died, they hired professional mourners. This was a big business in Palestine and you could make a lot of money being a professional mourner for people who had lost a loved one.

So Jesus walked into the place where Jairus' house was, and all around the perimeter were these loud, professional mourners, along with them some of the family members. And He simply told them to stop it.

The Dynamic Miracle

When Jesus told everyone that "the child is not dead, but sleeping," they ridiculed Him!

Jesus wasn't trying to discount the fact that this girl was dead— she was dead. But in Jesus' words, she was just sleeping. In the New Testament, that is the term that is used for people who know Jesus. When they die, their bodies just go to sleep.

Thirteen times in the New Testament, that reference is made to those who have died as Christians. Nevertheless, they ridiculed Him. He knew they had no faith whatsoever, so He sent them outside. And now to an audience of five—the mother, the father, and the three disciples—Jesus is going to perform an incredible miracle. Watch what He does in verses 41 and 42:

Then He took the child by the hand, and said to her, "Talitha, cumi," which is translated, "Little girl, I say to you, arise." Immediately the girl arose and walked, for she was twelve years of age. And they were overcome with great amazement.

In the New Testament record, there are only three occasions where Jesus brought somebody back from the dead: Jairus' daughter, the widow of Nain's son (Luke 7:11-17), and Lazarus (John 11:1-44). Jairus' daughter had just died before she was resurrected, the widow's son was being carried out to be buried before he was resurrected, and Lazarus had been dead for four days.

These three miracles of Jesus are included in the Gospels so that they demonstrate the totality of Jesus' ability to overcome death. A little girl, a young man, an adult—dead for a short time, dead for a little bit longer, dead for four days. None of it makes any difference when you know the Lord is in the house. He is in charge, and He has power over death.

Notes

1. R. Kent Hughes, *Mark, Volume 1: Jesus, Servant and Savior* (Wheaton, IL: Crossway Books, 1989), 126.

2. N. T. Wright, *Mark for Everyone* (Louisville, KY: Westminster John Knox Press, 2004), 61.

1. Read Mark 5:21-31.

   a. After crossing the Sea of Galilee once again, what was waiting for Jesus on the shore? (verse 21)

   b. What was the name of the man who came to Jesus? (verse 22) What was his job?

   c. What was the problem that this man had? What did he specifically want Jesus to do, believing that He could do it? (verse 23)

   d. What was Jesus' response to this request? What does the scene look like as they proceed? (verse 24)

   e. In verse 25 we find the second person needing a touch from Jesus. What was the woman's problem? How long had she suffered?

   f. What had doctors done for her condition? (verse 26)

   g. What was her reasoning for touching Jesus' garment? (verse 28)

   h What two things happened when she touched Jesus? (verse 29)

   i. What physical sensation did Jesus feel when she touched Him? (verse 30)

j. Why did the disciples think it was ridiculous for Jesus to want to know who touched Him? (verse 31)

2. Read Mark 5:31-43.

   a. When Jesus turned to look at the woman, write down the reaction she had and what actions she took. (verse 33)

   b. Jesus responded by saying that what had healed her? (verse 34)

   c. While He was healing that woman, what news made its way through the crowd? (verse 35)

   d. What was Jesus' response to this news? (verse 36)

   e. What did the scene at Jairus' house look like? (verse 38)

   f. What did Jesus say to those who were grieving? How did they respond to Him? (verses 39-40)

   g. How did Jesus go about performing this miracle? (verses 40-41)

   h. Jesus gave them two commands after the girl was brought back to life. (verse 43) What is striking about these two commands?

GROUP QUESTIONS

1. Read Psalm 103:1-5. Answer and discuss the following questions.

   a. This Psalm gives us five benefits that the Lord blesses us with. List them.

   b. Discuss with your group how you personally have experienced this benefit in your life.

   c. The psalmist says that these are reasons why we should bless the Lord. What keeps us from remembering these benefits? From giving God the glory He is due?

2. The woman in verse 25 had her illness for twelve years and the little girl who died was twelve years old. Talk about what is remarkable about the contrast between these two individuals and the time that binds them together.

3. When Jesus turned to look at the woman who had been healed by faith, her response was with "fearing and trembling." Do we react that way to Jesus? Should we? Discuss why or why not.

DID YOU KNOW?

The only statue known to be made of Jesus during His lifetime was erected because of the testimony of the woman with the issue of blood. After her healing, she returned to her hometown of Caesarea Philippi, an area found today in northeast Israel on the Golan Heights. Her testimony was so powerful that the community decided to create a monument to honor this miraculous work of God. In his book *Ecclesiastical History*, fourth-century Christian historian Eusebius described the statue as representing the moment when the woman touched the hem of Jesus' garment. And at that time, it still stood! But it has since been destroyed and lost to time.

HOW TO RESPOND TO REJECTION

Mark 6:1-13

In this lesson we observe the rejection of Jesus by the people of His very own hometown.

OUTLINE

Throughout the Gospel accounts there are numerous descriptions of the massive crowds who came to see Jesus and, in faith, be healed by Him. But when Jesus went to His own hometown of Nazareth, the reception and response He received was far different. They couldn't see Him as the Savior He truly was, only as a boy who grew up in that town.

I. **The Rejection of Jesus' Message**
   A. Jesus Preaching With Authority
   B. Jesus Provoking Astonishment
   C. Jesus Producing Anger
   D. Jesus Providing an Answer
   E. Jesus Prohibiting Any More Miracles

II. **The Rejection of Jesus' Men**
   A. Jesus Commissions His Disciples
   B. Jesus Commands His Disciples
   C. Jesus Circulates His Disciples

Have you ever felt rejected? It is one of the most hurtful feelings you can ever experience. And being rejected by your family is at the core of depression and despair for many people. Perhaps you have experienced that yourself. But just know this: You are not alone.

When you go to the Lord with your problems, you may wonder if He really understands what you are going through. Well, when you go to the Lord with the pain of being rejected, you are no doubt talking to someone who understands. Of all the people who ever walked on this earth, who you have ever read about in history, Jesus Christ experienced rejection at the deepest level.

In Isaiah 53:3, the rejection of Jesus was accurately prophesied: "He is despised and rejected by men, a Man of sorrows and acquainted with grief . . . we did not esteem Him."

We often think that Jesus' rejection began with the Holy Week events that led to the Cross. But if you follow the life of the Lord as it is replayed in the Gospels, you will discover that the trail of rejection He faced started early and went long, ultimately culminating at the Cross.

For instance, in Luke's Gospel we are told about an incident that occurred when Jesus was in His hometown of Nazareth. After speaking in the synagogue, those who "heard these things, were filled with wrath, and rose up and thrust Him out of the city; and they led Him to the brow of the hill on which their city was built, that they might throw Him down over the cliff" (Luke 4:28-29). When Jesus' own family heard about His ministry and miracles, they said, "He is out of His mind" (Mark 3:21). His own family thought Jesus was crazy!

Rejection was a part of Jesus' experience going all the way back to the earliest chapters in the Gospels. In Mark 6, we have perhaps the signature experience of the rejection of Jesus. We are going to methodically examine this passage and outline what happened to Him on this particular day.

THE REJECTION OF JESUS' MESSAGE

First of all, they rejected Jesus' message. John 1:11 says, "He came to His own, and His own did not receive Him." Let's explore an example of how people rejected the good news that Jesus presented about Himself.

Jesus Preaching With Authority

Mark 6:1-2 tells us that Jesus "came to His own country, and His disciples followed Him. And when the Sabbath had come, He began to teach in the synagogue." Up to this point in the book of Mark, most events have been centered in Capernaum, which had become Jesus' adopted home during His Galilean ministry. But now Jesus is going to visit Nazareth, His childhood hometown, the place where He had grown up.

When He arrived in Nazareth, He went to the synagogue on the Sabbath day and began to teach from the Scriptures. Gathered in the synagogue that day were members of His family and many who had known Him as a little boy running around the streets of Nazareth.

The news of His popularity had no doubt preceded Him. You could not have lived in that region without having heard of what was going on with Jesus—that people were flocking to see and hear Him not only from the area around Galilee but from across the borders. In fact, the crowds were so great that He often had to escape by means of a boat to the other side of the Sea of Galilee.

Curiosity about this young Man who was becoming known in the world was rampant in Nazareth as everyone stretched to see Him as He walked down the streets that day to the synagogue. He came preaching, and preaching with authority.

Jesus Provoking Astonishment

Jesus' preaching created quite a reaction: "And many hearing Him were astonished, saying, 'Where did this Man get these things? And what wisdom is this which is given to Him, that such mighty works are performed by His hands!'" (verse 2)

People were not prepared for the incredible wisdom and integrity that was coming out of the mouth of this Man that they thought they knew so well. They could not imagine how He had come to be what He was. They had watched Him grow up and there had never been anything about Him that would have led them to believe that He would turn out like this!

Jesus Producing Anger

The crowd did not stay in awe for long, saying, "'Is this not the carpenter, the Son of Mary, and brother of James, Joses, Judas, and Simon? And are not His sisters here with us?' So, they were offended at Him" (verse 3). How do you go from astonishment to anger? Well, it had to percolate a little bit in their minds. They were offended at Him; literally, they were "scandalized" by Jesus. They found Him too much for them, or perhaps more to the point, they rejected Him.

Their response was full of cynicism and sarcasm. First, they refer to Him as "the carpenter." Only Mark uses this expression concerning Jesus, but it proves that for thirty years the Lord was not ashamed to be a carpenter. He worked with His hands.

The citizens of Nazareth, however, viewed Him as nothing more than a common laborer. They believed that due to His background, He had no right to be teaching them. It was a very mean-spirited description.

They also called Jesus "the Son of Mary." This was a cheap shot because their fathers, not their mothers, always identified sons even if their father was dead. They were implying that Jesus was the illegitimate offspring of this woman.[1] This form of ridicule and rejection must have hurt deeply.

Finally, they also brought up His brothers and sisters. They were obviously present that day in the synagogue when Jesus was teaching. And the crowd was angry that Jesus presumed to elevate Himself above His own family. How dare He think that He is better than His four brothers and His two sisters?

Jesus Providing an Answer

Jesus responded to all these questions and accusations by saying in verse 4, "A prophet is not without honor except in his own country, among his own relatives, and in his own house." This is just another way of saying that familiarity breeds contempt. Jesus was so close to them that they did not see Him.

But how could they have missed Him? As John Phillips put it,

He never quarreled, never lost His temper, never told lies, and never acted selfishly. He was never disobedient, never discourteous, and never moody. They were so accustomed to His absolute goodness and its marvelous unobtrusiveness that they failed even to see it.[2]

How would you not notice somebody like that? Jesus was consistently, absolutely, completely, and without exception, totally good. But His humility was such that He did not wear it on His sleeve. He just lived it in His life. And somehow the people who grew up with Him in those early years, they missed it all! So, when He came back, they rejected Him.

Jesus Prohibiting Any More Miracles

Because of their skepticism, Jesus walked away from Nazareth, doing no more miracles in their city. Mark 6:5-6 says, "Now He could do no mighty work there, except that He laid His hands on a few sick people and healed them. And He marveled because of their unbelief. Then He went about the villages in a circuit, teaching."

Due to the unbelief of the people in the synagogue of Nazareth that day, Jesus was prohibited from doing any more miracles. It wasn't that He couldn't—it was that He wouldn't. Their unbelief was so strong that Jesus was amazed by it. He marveled at their lack of faith. Only twice in the New Testament did Jesus marvel at something. He marveled at the centurion (Matthew 8:10), and He marveled at the unbelief in His hometown.[3]

Unbelief hinders the work of Christ. Is there anything that God cannot do? Yes, there is. In a sense, God's work is hindered by the unbelief of His people. God tells us that Jesus could not do many miracles there. Why? Because the people did not believe.

In our culture today—and even in our churches—God is limited by the unbelief of His people, by their unwillingness to take steps of faith. There is no faith without risk. A church and a people that want to be honored and blessed by God must be willing to step out by faith and believe that God will open the way for them.

In Luke 17:5, the apostles pled to Jesus, "Increase our faith." And in Mark 9:24, a man cried out to Jesus, "Lord, I believe; help my unbelief!" That should always be our prayer. God has given us faith to believe great things so that God can do great things.

But that day in Nazareth, the people there shut God down. Let us commit ourselves that such a thing will never be said of us, that we will never turn away from what God wants to do because we do not trust and believe in Him.

THE REJECTION OF JESUS' MEN

Now Jesus is going to pull together His own experience of rejection with a warning to His followers that they can expect the same thing to happen in their own lives.

Jesus Commissions His Disciples

In verse 7, Jesus "called the twelve to Himself, and began to send them out two by two, and gave them power over unclean spirits." Since the Lord Jesus could no longer do any miracles in Nazareth, He determined to multiply Himself by sending out the twelve. He sent out six teams and gave each of them His own power. He enabled them to preach the Gospel and gave them power to cast out demons and to heal the sick.

Jesus' act of commissioning and sending the men out two by two establishes a pattern in the New Testament. Just consider these ministry teams: Peter and John, Barnabas and Paul, Barnabas and Mark, Paul and Silas. This is God's method, allowing iron to sharpen iron. God never intended for us to do this alone. He wants us to do it together with partners, to be dynamic duos for God.

Jesus Commands His Disciples

Next, Jesus gives His disciples some interesting instructions. He submits two commands that are very intriguing when you take the time to examine them.

1. The Command About Simplicity

Jesus' first command regards having very simple means as they traveled: "He commanded them to take nothing for the journey except a staff—no bag, no bread, no copper in their money belts— but to wear sandals, and not to put on two tunics" (Mark 6:8-9).

Jesus essentially told them not to take anything with them. They were not to pack a suitcase or to take money for provisions. Nobody would do that today!

Jesus sent His disciples out just as they were. These original marching orders were very appropriate for that time. The people whose paths they crossed would take care of them. And many would not only open their homes, but they would open their hearts. The Lord wanted this to be a blessing both for the disciples (seeing how God would provide for them) and also for the people who were given the privilege of sincere hospitality.

Here's a word about simplicity: Even though we are sophisticated today in what we do with all the tools we have, God does not need them at all. Just take a trip to the mission field and see how God still gets His work done without all the stuff we so quickly accumulate along the way. All He needs is a dedicated person with a clear message—and He can change the world.

2. The Command About Hospitality

Secondly, Jesus sent them out with a word of hospitality. He said to them, "In whatever place you enter a house, stay there till you depart from that place. And whoever will not receive you nor hear you, when you depart from there, shake off the dust under your feet as a testimony against them" (Mark 6:10-11).

The disciples were to depend on the hospitality of those to whom they went to minister. If they went into a little village, they were to identify someone and explain that they had come in the name of the Lord to preach the Gospel. And the Bible says they were not to leave, but to stay in one place and minister to the community until it was time for them to leave the city.

But if they were rejected by the city, they were simply to shake the dust off their sandals "as a testimony against them." This Jewish custom was often practiced when Jewish people would cross over into Gentile territory. The Jews felt the Gentiles were unworthy, so if they had to cut across the corner of a Gentile piece of property, as they got to the edge of that land they would shake the dust off their shoes as a sign that it was unworthy.

This is a great lesson for us when it comes to rejection. Everybody is rejected sometimes.

But rejection only lasts a moment. The only thing you can do about it is how you respond to it. So just shake the dust off your feet!

Don't make it the purpose for the rest of your life to get even with somebody who has rejected you. Just get your eye on the goal, stay focused on the purpose, and get the Gospel out to as many people as you can. Not everybody is going to receive it—some people didn't even receive Jesus!

Jesus Circulates His Disciples

After Jesus gave the disciples all of this information, "they went out and preached that people should repent. And they cast out many demons, and anointed with oil many who were sick, and healed them." What were they doing? Exactly what Jesus had been doing! Jesus had now replicated Himself in six teams who were out doing everything He was doing.

Being rejected Himself, He prepared them for rejection as He sent them out to do His work in His Name. The most wonderful thing to think about, though, is that we will never be rejected by the Lord. Will rejection in our human life ever go away? No, but we have been accepted by God, and the good, good news is that God is continually accepting people into His family.

Notes

1. R. Kent Hughes, *Mark, Volume 1: Jesus, Servant and Savior* (Wheaton, IL: Crossway Books, 1989), 210.

2. John Phillips, *Exploring the Gospel of Mark* (Grand Rapids, MI: Kregel, 2003), 113.

3. E. Schuyler English, *Studies in the Gospel According to Mark* (NY: Arno C. Gaebelein, Inc., 1943), 164.

PERSONAL QUESTIONS

1. Read Mark 6:1-6.

   a. After His many travels, where is Jesus found in this passage? (verse 1)

   b. What did Jesus proceed to do on the Sabbath? (verse 2)

   c. The crowd was initially astonished by what three aspects of Jesus' teaching? (verse 2)

   d. They then proceeded to point out what aspects of Jesus? (verse 3)

   e. Once they labeled Him in those terms, how did they react to Jesus? (verse 3)

   f. Paraphrase Jesus' response in verse 4 to their unbelief.

   g. Because of their unbelief, what incredible fact is given in verse 5?

h. How did Jesus respond to this treatment? (verse 6)

2. Read Mark 6:7-13.

   a. As He paired up the disciples, what power did Jesus give them? (verse 7)

   b. Jesus gave them specific instructions to not travel with what three things? (verse 8)

   c. What were the only two items they could bring with them? (verses 8-9)

   d. What simple action were they to take if they were not received? What would the result of this simple action be? (verse 11)

   e. The disciples preached repentance and did what three acts in Jesus' Name? (verse 13)

1. Read Matthew 19:16-22.

   a. What question did the rich young ruler have for Jesus? Was this a good question? Discuss.

   b. What is remarkable about the young man's response to Jesus quoting some of the Ten Commandments to him?

   c. What did Jesus then tell the young man in verse 21 that proved to be a bridge too far for him?

   d. In verse 22, Jesus did not chase down the young man but let him walk away. Think about the ramifications of that. What is your response to the reality that Jesus allows some people to walk away from Him?

2. Read Matthew 21:42-45.

   a. Jesus quotes Psalm 118:22-23 in verse 42. How does that relate to Jesus and the passage we just read?

   b. Verses 43-44 contain some very strong words from Jesus about those who deny Him. Talk about His words. Are you thankful for them? Are you a recipient of them?

3. Read John 1:10-13.

   a. How do verses 10-11 relate to Jesus' experience in Nazareth? In Jerusalem? In the world today?

   b. What happens to those who believe in the Name of Jesus? (verse 12)

c. What three things are the children of God not born of? What are they born of? (verse 13) Why should this fact not be missed by Christians and non-Christians alike?

DID YOU KNOW?

Nazareth is a city with a fascinating history and is a place that can still be visited today. Nazareth was the hometown of Mar, and was the site of Gabriel's announcement that she would bear the Savior of the world (Luke 1:26). In Jesus' day, it was a small, Jewish village with probably 400 to 500 residents. Modern Nazareth is the largest Arab city in Israel, with more than 75,000 residents in its greater area. Even though it is considered to be the Arab capital of Israel, it is still home to many Christians (about 30 percent of the population) who oversee the churches that were built on the many historic sites that are recorded in the Bible.

THE GREATEST MAN WHO EVER LIVED

Mark 6:14-29

In this lesson we witness the testimony and death of John the Baptist.

OUTLINE

Do you consider yourself a religious person? Many people do because they have a worldview and practices that include (or may not include) "God." While Christianity is often called a religion, it is not. Rather, it is a relationship that brings new life rather than reforming the old.

I. Herod's Memory of John the Baptist

II. Herod's Murder of John the Baptist
   A. The Incarceration of John the Baptist
   B. The Indictment by John the Baptist
   C. The Indignation Toward John the Baptist
   D. The Intimidation of John the Baptist
   E. The Intrigue Against John the Baptist
   F. The Immediate Execution of John the Baptist
   G. The Interment of John the Baptist

Conclusion: Why the Story of John the Baptist?
   1. To Remind Us That Discipleship Is Dangerous
   2. To Remind Us That Death Has Been Defeated

I n the late 1940s, a strange young preacher dressed in a pistachio-colored suit with a flaming red tie and who spoke in a pronounced Southern accent had an incredible impact on all those who came to hear him—he drew thousands upon thousands to his crusades. His name was Billy Graham. In the late twenties of the first century, John the Baptist created a similar stir.

Like Billy Graham, John the Baptist was also a young man in his early thirties, and he dressed and spoke differently than anyone else did at the time. And like Billy Graham, he drew large crowds with his preaching for repentance. To top it all off, Jesus Christ said that John the Baptist was the greatest man who ever lived.

In John 5:35, Jesus called John the Baptist a "burning and shining lamp." But the term for "burning and shining lamp" actually translates better as being like a wick on a candle. What does Jesus mean here then? Well, a wick is something that is consumed when it is functioning. John the Baptist was consumed by his message. He came into this world for a purpose and that purpose literally consumed him, and then he disappeared.

Other than Jesus Christ, there is more written about the birth of John the Baptist than any other person in the New Testament. He was a man with a special mission. And even though he only ministered for about a year in public, he was a great man in his ministry. But as we're going to learn in this study, he was also a great man in his death.

When Jesus Christ started His dynamic preaching and healing ministry in the Galilean region, the word of His fame began to spread. He became an international celebrity. People came from Jerusalem and from outside of Israel to hear Jesus speak. And His crowds were growing.

Word about Jesus and the crowds that came to listen to Him and to see the miracles He performed reached Herod's palace, and ultimately Herod heard about it. This particular Herod was Herod Antipas. He was the second son of Herod the Great, and he ruled Galilee from 4 B.C. until he was banished in A.D. 39. Like all of the Herods, he was a wicked and cruel tyrant.

When Herod heard about Jesus' popularity, he thought that somehow John the Baptist had come back to life! What a testimony to John that someone would confuse him for the Savior of the world. Herod tries to deal with the mystery of who Jesus is and with the memory of who he knows John is.

HEROD'S MEMORY OF JOHN THE BAPTIST

When Herod Antipas heard about Jesus, he also heard what others were saying about Him. People made claims about who Jesus was (Elijah, etc.), but Herod was certain that he knew better. He had never heard of anyone with the power and charisma that Jesus supposedly had with the exception of one man—and that man was John the Baptist.

And for reasons we're about to discover, Herod was haunted by the memory of John the Baptist. He was absolutely certain that John had come back to life and was back on the scene in his domain. That is why Herod said of Jesus in verse 16, "This is John, whom I beheaded; he has been raised from the dead!"

HEROD'S MURDER OF JOHN THE BAPTIST

Herod was responsible for the death of John the Baptist and that evil act was something that haunted him every day of his life. Let's look at the events leading up to his murder.

The Incarceration of John the Baptist

The story of John the Baptist's murder is the only story in the entire Gospel of Mark that is not centered on Jesus Christ. Verse 17 describes the circumstances of his incarceration: "For Herod himself had sent and laid hold of John, and bound him in prison for the sake of Herodias, his brother Philip's wife; for he had married her."

Herod put John the Baptist in prison for publicly denouncing his adulterous marriage to his brother's wife. But Herodias was not who he thought she was. Once he married her, Herod discovered who she truly was for she was wicked—even more wicked than he was! More than one writer has referred to her as the Jezebel of the New Testament.

The Indictment by John the Baptist

John had been placed in prison because he had the courage to tell Herod, "It is not lawful for you to have your brother's wife" (verse 18). When John heard about Herod stealing his own brother's wife, Herodias, and marrying her, he went into the presence of the king and told him that what he had done was sinful, immoral, and wrong.

Herod couldn't have been too happy about that accusation, but he was not nearly as unhappy as Herodias was. She took great offense to John the Baptist making such a pronouncement about their royal marriage. Herod didn't want anything to happen to John because, as we're going to see later, he was intrigued by the man John the Baptist.

And so, rather than punish him by killing him, Herod simply put him in prison. The public ministry of John the Baptist lasted less than one year, but his influence was extraordinary because he became the private prisoner of the king—King Herod.

The Indignation Toward John the Baptist

In verse 19 we learn that "Herodias held it against him and wanted to kill him, but she could not." Herodias hated John for telling her that her marriage was wrong. As far as she was concerned, it was none of John the Baptist's business.

She was furious at John, but she was also angry at her husband because he wouldn't punish John appropriately. Under normal circumstances, anyone who had made such an accusation against the king would have lost their life. But Herod did not want to kill John the Baptist, so he gave him a lenient sentence.

Herodias wanted John to die, but Herod would not agree to this ultimate punishment! As long as Herod had control of the prison, he wouldn't let his wife kill this man. At this point in the story, John had been in prison for almost a whole year. All this time, Herodias has been waiting for a chance to get even with John the Baptist. She was not going to quit until he was vanquished in her eyes, and that meant his death.

The Intimidation of John the Baptist

John the Baptist's testimony must have made a powerful impact on Herod because in verse 20 we are told "Herod feared John" (verse 20). Here is the interesting thing: Instead of John the Baptist being afraid of Herod—Herod was afraid of John!

Why was he afraid of John? Because John was a holy and godly man. John the Baptist maintained his stand for righteousness regardless of whether he was with a friend or someone who could ultimately take his life. He was a man of great courage. Herod was afraid because he saw the power of God on John's life.

In fact, the Bible says that because of his relationship with John the Baptist, Herod did "many things." What that means is he changed the way he lived his life. And Herod also "heard him gladly."

Apparently, Herod would periodically go and have John the Baptist summoned out of the dungeon and have him preach a sermon. John the Baptist would preach to Herod! And because he spoke the truth no matter who was there to hear it, he gained the respect of the one man who had power over his life.

But Herod's admiration of John was not equal to Herod's fear of Herodias. And here lies the problem: Herod was more afraid of his wife than he was of John.

The Intrigue Against John the Baptist

John the Baptist's whole situation is about to change in a moment of intrigue. He is finally going to be caught in the snare of Herodias' hate, and it all unfolds at a party. At this party, Herod will make a promise that he will regret, and John the Baptist's fate will be sealed.

According to secular history, Herodias' daughter was a girl named Salome. The book of Mark tells us that she danced before Herod to celebrate his birthday. Whatever that dance was, it was powerful enough for Herod to say, "Ask me whatever you want, and I will give it to you . . . . up to half my kingdom."

Herod's promise here was foolish. First of all, he did not have the right to give his kingdom away because he didn't have a kingdom —he was simply ruling on behalf of Rome. Secondly, his vow was foolish because he made the promise in the presence of his aristocratic friends and nobles. He was stuck! He couldn't go back now on his word or he would lose face in front of this assemblage. Herod was trapped, and because he was trapped, John was doomed.

As soon as Salome heard the promise from Herod, her first thought was to run to her mother and ask her what to do. For Herodias, this was a no-brainer. This was the moment she had been waiting for. This was her opportunity to get her husband to do what he had refused to do up until this point. Finally, she would have her revenge on John the Baptist.

The Immediate Execution of John the Baptist

The grisly execution of John the Baptist is marked by four heinous acts.

1. The Hideous Request

In verse 25 we read Salome's gruesome response to the king's promise: "I want you to give me at once the head of John the Baptist on a platter." Here they were at a feast with platters of food all around. And now Salome wants not food, but the head of John the Baptist on a platter.

Notice in the text that three words are used one after the other: "immediately," "with haste," and "at once." Herodias instructed her daughter to go and ask for this to be done immediately. Why would she ask that? Because she was afraid that when her husband got sober, he would change his mind or figure out a way to go back on his promise. So John's death could not wait until the morning—it had to happen that night.

2. The Haunting Remorse

Herod's remorse is evident in verse 26: "And the king was exceedingly sorry; yet, because of the oaths and because of those who sat with him, he did not want to refuse her". As we pointed out earlier, Herod himself had been trapped by his own words. There was nothing he could do but carry out the gruesome request.

3. The Hurried Response

The response is hurried, for in verse 27 we read: "Immediately the king sent an executioner and commanded his head to be brought. And he went and beheaded him in prison." Herodias' dream had come true. The vengeance she sought was hers.

4. The Horrible Result

Then in verse 28 the horrible scene is depicted for us, saying: They "brought his head on a platter, and gave it to the girl; and the girl gave it to her mother." What a grizzly story!

The Interment of John the Baptist

The end of John the Baptist is detailed in verse 29: "When his disciples heard of it, they came and took away his corpse and laid it in a tomb." Thus ends the life of John the Baptist and the description of his ministry in the text. But we must ask this: Why is this narrative placed at this particular point in the book of Mark?

CONCLUSION: WHY THE STORY OF JOHN THE BAPTIST?

Just before the account of John the Baptist, Mark tells us that the Lord Jesus sent out His disciples, two by two to do the work of ministry. And what was their ministry? To cast out demons, to heal the sick, and to preach the Gospel.

Immediately after the story of John the Baptist in the book of Mark, the disciples return with their report of what happened as they went out doing the work of the Lord. Sandwiched in between those two events is the story of John the Baptist and his execution.

Why is the book of Mark constructed like that? There are two very important reasons why.

To Remind Us That Discipleship Is Dangerous

The story of John the Baptist is placed where it is in the Gospel of Mark to remind us that discipleship is dangerous. We often have an ethereal idea about what it means to be a follower of Jesus, that it's all "pie in the sky, by and by," but to be a disciple of Jesus is a costly calling.

Jesus was rejected by His own family, and the disciples were told that they would also be cast out of some cities and rejected because the Gospel wouldn't be received by all. And then John the Baptist is killed for his blatant honesty about sexual morality.

Jesus had just instructed His disciples to go out and do miracles. And He had given them a message to preach that would draw crowds. But in the midst of all of this excitement about the joys of the ministry, the Lord God deposited in their hearts a reminder that discipleship is dangerous. Discipleship is costly.

To Remind Us That Death Has Been Defeated

Secondly, John the Baptist's story is here to remind us that death has been defeated. Usually the hero in stories is not killed. And the power of evil in this story seems like it has won. But on the foundation of John's execution, twelve flaming evangelists are set loose with the Gospel in Galilee.[1]

Through the death of John the Baptist, there was a mighty movement among the disciples to take their roles more seriously. Those who knew John the Baptist went out after that experience with a greater zeal and urgency than they'd ever known before. John the Baptist might have died, but his message was living on. It was now embodied not in just one person, but in twelve.

John the Baptist lives on in our hearts as a brave man who was used of God for a brief moment as a burning and shining light to point men and women to Jesus. And that is what we've been called to do: to be burning and shining lights for the Gospel of Jesus Christ.

Note

1. David E. Garland, *The NIV Application Commentary: Mark* (Grand Rapids, MI: Zondervan, 1996), Kindle edition.

PERSONAL QUESTIONS

1. Read Mark 6:14-20.

   a. Jesus had become so well known that we are told what? (verse 14)

   b. Who did Herod think Jesus was? Why? (verse 14)

   c. What were some of the other common speculations of who Jesus really was? (verse 15)

   d. Herod thought Jesus was John, even though he had done what to John the Baptist? (verse 16)

e. Why did Herod imprison John the Baptist? (verses 17-18)

f. Who really wanted John the Baptist dead? (verse 19)

g. Why couldn't she kill John? (verse 20)

h. List the remarkable ways Herod felt and acted toward his prisoner. (verse 20)

2. Read Mark 6:21-29.

   a. What three manners of men were present at Herod's birthday party? (verse 21)

   b. Who danced for Herod? (verse 22)

   c. What was Herod's response to her dance? What was he willing to give her? (verses 22-23)

   d. Instead of giving Herod an answer right there, what did this young woman do? (verse 24)

   e. What did Herodias and her daughter end up asking for? (verses 24-25)

f. What was Herod's emotional response to this request? (verse 26)

g. Why did he go ahead and order a request that he didn't want to enact? (verse 26)

h. In the end, who ended up with the head of John the Baptist? (verse 28)

i. What did the disciples do with the rest of John's body? (verse 29)

GROUP QUESTIONS

1. Read Matthew 3:11-12 and discuss the following questions.

   a. Jesus said that John the Baptist was the greatest man who ever lived, but who did John say was greater than himself? What humble act did John the Baptist say he was not worthy of?

   b. What does John's humility and deference to Jesus demonstrate to you? Are we that reverential to Jesus today? If not, why not?

   c. What was John's purpose in baptizing people? What does he say that Jesus brings to baptism? Is that something widely taught today? Discuss.

d. Verse 12 shows a side of Jesus that people often don't like to discuss or acknowledge. Why do we ignore the Jesus of fire and cleansing?

2. Read Matthew 3:13-17.

   a. When Jesus came to be baptized by John, what was John's response? (verse 14)

   b. How did Jesus convince John to baptize Him considering what John knew about the true nature of Jesus? (verse 15)

c. What physically happened as Jesus came up out of the water? (verse 16)

d. What was heard after the baptism of Jesus? (verse 17)

e. Discuss why this is one of the most significant moments in Jesus' life and in the Bible.

DID YOU KNOW?

The location of John the Baptist's imprisonment and execution was a fortress on the eastern side of the Dead Sea called Machaerus. Roman historian Josephus tells us that the Machaerus prison was built in 30 B.C. by Herod the Great (he was Herod Antipas' father). Machaerus is similar in construction to Masada (another extravagant fortress/palace) because it was also built by Herod the Great—although Masada is found on the other side of the Dead Sea. You can visit the magnificent ruins and scene of John the Baptist's final days today in the country of Jordan, on the eastern border of Israel.

JESUS AND OUR PROBLEMS

Mark 6:30-44

In this lesson we observe one of Jesus' greatest miracles: the feeding of the five thousand.

OUTLINE

During His short time on the earth, Jesus performed many miracles of great variety and scope. But there is only one miracle that is recorded in all four Gospel accounts—Matthew, Mark, Luke, and John. Because of this great distinction, it is imperative that we take care to fully appreciate and analyze Jesus' feeding of the five thousand.

I. **Defining Our Problems**
   A. The Problem of Insufficient Time
   B. The Problem of an Inconvenient Place
   C. The Problem of Inadequate Resources

II. **Determining Our Possibilities**
   A. The Calloused Approach
   B. The Calculating Approach
   C. The Compassionate Approach

III. **Discovering Our Potential**

IV. **Developing Our Plan**
   A. Organizing the People
   B. Consecrating the Plan
   C. Administering the Program
   D. Evaluating the Progress

The feeding of the five thousand was a miracle used by the Lord Jesus Christ as a foundation upon which He would teach the important truth that there is another kind of food that we all need. Jesus multiplied the bread so that He could ultimately tell us about Himself—the Bread of Life.[1] As John 6:27 clearly states, "Do not labor for the food which perishes, but for the food which endures to everlasting life, which the Son of Man will give you, because God the Father has set His seal on Him."

While this miracle reminds us of God's miraculous power, it also teaches us that God does His best work through people. In this story we are going to meet Philip, Andrew, and all the other confused disciples. We are also going to meet a little boy who ended up playing a crucial role in this miracle. And we are finally going to see all of the disciples employed in making the result of this miracle available to the people who were hungry.

The feeding of the five thousand is a classic illustration of problem solving. In this study we are going to walk through the steps that Jesus took in solving the problem of the hungry masses. How do you deal with your problem? What is your philosophy of problem solving? How do you go about it?

DEFINING OUR PROBLEMS

This story begins with a problem that stems from the success of Jesus' ministry. He was drawing huge crowds, and on this particular day, Jesus instructed His disciples to follow Him to a little retreat where they might recover their energy. But the crowds already knew where Jesus was going!

Apparently, when they saw the direction of the boat, they realized, "Oh, Jesus is going there!" They somehow found a way to get there before Jesus and the disciples did. And the crowd only multiplied over time. In fact, we find out later there were at least fifteen thousand people in this crowd.

So for the entire day, Jesus and His disciples preached and ministered to these people. They had been out in the hot sun all day long. And remember, the disciples have just come off their first preaching tour. They didn't go and rest—they went and worked! Everyone on the scene—the disciples, the crowd—was incredibly hungry and tired.

So in John 6:5, we read, "Then Jesus lifted up His eyes, and seeing a great multitude coming toward Him, He said to Philip, 'Where shall we buy bread, that these may eat?'" Before anything could be done to solve the problem, the problem had to be understood. Every miracle that Jesus ever performed started with a problem that needed a solution.

Here is a good biblical definition of *problems*: Problems are situations engineered by God to bring us face to face with our deficiencies so that we might view His sufficiency as the only alternative. God allows problems in our lives so that we will be forced to come to God for the solution—which is where we should have been in the first place.

In this instance, Jesus identified three problems that had to be solved.

The Problem of Insufficient Time

First of all, we read in verse 35 that "the day was now far spent . . . and already the hour is late." On that particular day, time had run out. People could not be sent home for food; many of them had walked more than ten miles to this event!

The Problem of an Inconvenient Place

Secondly, we read that it was "a deserted place." Now please note that this is not the desert, for a little bit later on, we read about grass. It is not the desert; it is a deserted place. They were in an isolated and uninhabited location where food was not available. The day was almost over and there was no place to purchase or acquire food.

The Problem of Inadequate Resources

This problem becomes more impossible the more you know about it. Verse 44 tells us that "those who had eaten the loaves were about five thousand men." But Matthew adds this additional bit of information in his account: "Now those who had eaten were about five thousand men, besides women and children" (Matthew 14:21).

This is where we get the estimation of fifteen thousand people. For every man there must have been at least one woman and a child. That is a low estimation with the assumption of small families. So there had to have been at least fifteen thousand people gathered around Jesus.

The day was spent, there was no place to get food, and at least fifteen thousand people were hungry. This was an impossible situation!

Rather than relieve the crisis as He could have done in an instant, Jesus turned to His disciples and told them to give the people something to eat. You should have seen the look on their faces when He said that. To their minds this was an unreasonable, impossible request.[2]

When Jesus gave this direction, He most likely had a smile on His face. He knew what He was doing. He was purposely putting the disciples through a test.

God puts us through tests to see whether or not we really do believe in Him and trust Him. He wants us to come to Him first, not just as a last resort when all else fails. Many people try everything else and only resort to prayer as a last-ditch effort. Don't put it last —put it first!

DETERMINING OUR POSSIBILITIES

After you define the problems, you determine the possibilities. There are three possibilities that are previewed in this story; that is, three different ways of looking at this problem and how it can be solved.

The Calloused Approach

When Jesus tells the disciples to get the people some food, they reply in verse 36, "Send them away, that they may go into the surrounding country and villages and buy themselves bread." When Jesus said, "Give them something to eat," they turned around and said to Him, "No, You tell them to go home. We're not feeding this crowd."

They were not willing to take ownership of the problem. They thought the only answer was to send the people away and let them solve their own problem. The disciples just wanted to cynically ignore the problem and hope that the hungry people would go away.

The Calculating Approach

The calculating approach is given to us in the disciples' response in verse 37: "Shall we go and buy two hundred denarii worth of bread and give them something to eat?" In John's Gospel, we are given even more pertinent information: "But this He said to test him, for He Himself knew what He would do. Philip answered Him, 'Two hundred denarii worth of bread is not sufficient for them, that every one of them may have a little'" (John 6:6-7).

Jesus addressed Philip with this question because Philip came from the neighboring town of Bethsaida (John 1:44). If anyone knew the area, it would be Philip. So Jesus looked at Philip and said: "Philip, you live around here. Where can we find enough food to feed fifteen thousand people?"

Now, it is important to know that Philip was like an accountant. So he began to punch in the numbers, and his calculations didn't add up. A denarii was one day's wages for one man, and Philip said that it would take two hundred days of work just to get to the edge of the hunger of these people—and even that would not be enough.

When the Lord Jesus asked Philip that question, He asked him to test him. His question was clearly designed to set a predicament before Philip that had no human solution. He was enabling Philip to realize that there was no practical or pragmatic way of solving this problem.

The Compassionate Approach

But there is one last approach to solving the problem, and it involves the Savior. Matthew 14:14 tells us that "when Jesus went out He saw a great multitude; and He was moved with compassion for them." The word *compassion* here is an incredible word that has its root in the ancient Greek language, the meaning "viscera" or "stomach."[3]

There is no Greek word for *heart*, so in that day whenever they tried to talk about what we today would say is your heart, they would say one of two things: either your stomach or your kidneys —the inward part of you. So when the Bible says that Jesus walked out and saw all these people with nothing to eat, He was filled with compassion for them in the very core of His being.

DISCOVERING OUR POTENTIAL

The disciples complain about what they don't have, but Jesus focuses rather on what they do have. In fact, the problem will not be resolved by something beyond them, but by something from among them. Jesus sees possibilities where the disciples only see impossibilities. But Jesus knows that God can take even the smallest thing and multiply it into enough so that it can take care of many. Little is much when God is in it.

In verse 38, Jesus asked, "How many loaves do you have? Go and see." The result was meager: "Five, and two fish." There are some additional details found in John 6:9: "There is a lad here who has five barley loaves and two small fish, but what are they among so many?"

Andrew had been looking around, and he found a little boy in this huge crowd who was ready to have his lunch. Apparently, his mother had prepared this for him, a small lunch of bread and fish. And just like Philip, Andrew had done some calculations. That is why he said to Jesus, "What are they among so many?" Imagine comparing this little bit of food Andrew found with the incredible need that had presented itself.

DEVELOPING OUR PLAN

There are four components to Jesus' development of His plan.

Organizing the People

Jesus begins by giving directions. He "commanded them to make them all sit down in groups on the green grass. So they sat down in ranks, in hundreds and in fifties" (verses 39-40). After Jesus receives the loaves (He hasn't done anything with them yet), He prepares for the food to be distributed. Despite the scant resources, Jesus ordered the crowd to sit down in groups of such size that will make it manageable to serve the crowd once He performs the miracle.[4]

Consecrating the Plan

Then, in verse 41, Jesus consecrates His plan: "And when He had taken the five loaves and the two fish, He looked up to heaven, blessed and broke the loaves." Can you imagine asking God's blessing on the food when there is no food? But when He prayed, Jesus thanked God for something He had not yet received. He prayed for the food that He could see—the loaves and the fishes—and for the food that He couldn't see but that was about to be distributed.

Administering the Program

After the prayer, Jesus took the loaves and fish "and gave them to His disciples to set before them; and the two fish He divided among them all" (verse 41). The miracle hasn't happened yet. Jesus just took the fish and loaves and distributed it in equal parts to the twelve disciples. Nothing has happened yet.

Evaluating the Progress

The result of the miracle being performed was displayed in three unique ways:

1. The People Were Satisfied

Verses 42 and 43 tell us, "So they all ate and were filled. And they took up twelve baskets full of fragments and of the fish." So what happened? Every time the disciples took something out of the basket and gave it to someone, there was more to be found in the basket. Every time they gave something away, it was replenished.

No matter how much they gave away, there was always more. And that went on until every one of the fifteen thousand people had enough to eat and twelve baskets were left over. And then it didn't happen anymore!

2. The Savior Was Glorified

John 6:14 shows us the response: "Then those men, when they had seen the sign that Jesus did, said, 'This is truly the Prophet who is to come into the world.'" Though their observation was incomplete, they at least began to recognize that Jesus was someone who was unique and special.

Perhaps they remembered Moses and the manna from heaven, or Elijah who was fed at the brook by ravens. They are beginning to realize that Jesus is a divine Prophet, and the Savior is getting glorified in this.

3. The Principle Was Magnified

The principle that explains the miracle is this: the principle of giving. The young boy gave to Andrew and then the disciples gave the food to Jesus. Jesus then gave the provisions to the disciples, and the disciples distributed it to the multitudes. A contagion of giving took place. The more that was given, the more there was to give. When giving took place, God moved within the affairs of men and released His power.

The disciples didn't have much to give, but that is never the point. The point is that what they did give was enough to move the mightiness of God into the scene and demonstrate how man's little becomes much under the right circumstances.

It is not about what you don't have; it is about what you do have. It is not about what you can't give; it is about what you can give. When we give what God has entrusted to us, God takes that which is little and makes it big. Only God can do that.

Notes

1. Warren Wiersbe, *Be Diligent* (Colorado Springs, CO: David C. Cook, 1987), 80-81.

2. James R. Edwards, *The Gospel According to Mark* (Grand Rapids, MI: Wm. B. Eerdmans, 2002), Kindle edition.

3. R. Kent Hughes, *Mark, Volume 1: Jesus, Servant and Savior* (Wheaton, IL: Crossway Books, 1989), 148-49.

4. James R. Edwards, *The Gospel According to Mark* (Grand Rapids, MI: Wm. B. Eerdmans, 2002), Kindle edition.

1. Read Mark 6:30-37.

    a. Why did Jesus suggest that the disciples get some rest? (verse 31)

    b. Where did they endeavor to go to get some peace and quiet? (verse 32)

    c. How were their plans for rest thwarted? How did the people find them? (verse 33)

    d. Where did all the people come from? What remarkable detail is given to us at the end of verse 33?

e. Instead of being annoyed at the scene, why was Jesus moved when He looked out at the great crowd? (verse 34)

f. Why were the disciples intent on sending the people away? (verses 35-36)

g. What was Jesus' pointed response to their request? (verse 37)

2. Read Mark 6:37-44.

   a. What was the disciples' excuse for not feeding this huge crowd? (verse 37)

b. Jesus took their complaint and asked them to do what instead? (verse 38)

c. What provisions were they able to find? (verse 38)

d. How did Jesus organize the crowd prior to the feeding? (verses 39-40)

e. Before He divided the provisions, what was Jesus careful to do? (verse 41)

f. What was the end result of Jesus' actions? (verses 42-43)

g. Why is the author of Mark careful to say that five thousand *men* were fed in verse 44?

1. Read Isaiah 55:1-2.

   a. How does verse 1 relate to some things that Jesus said about Himself? Find three quotes from Jesus that are similar in theme to this verse and write them below.

   b. Instead of spending our money and time on what does not satisfy, what are we instructed to do in verse 2?

   c. This passage, as well as the feeding of the five thousand, is about the Lord's abundance. Why do we then strive to do things in our own way and in our own power? Discuss.

2. Read John 6:32-36.

   a. Jesus disputes the Pharisees assertion about Moses and
      manna by saying what instead? (verse 32)

   b. The bread of God, the bread of life, is marked by what two
      things? (verse 33)

   c. What radical claims does Jesus make in verse 35 to show the
      unbelieving nature of the Pharisees?

d. Jesus said in verse 36 that the Pharisees saw Him, yet did not believe. What keeps people from wanting the bread of life, from wanting salvation?

3. Time and time again, Jesus was attentive to the real physical needs of people. What does that say about a holy God who condescends to care about our daily needs like hunger and thirst?

DID YOU KNOW?

It is always helpful, when possible, to read the accounts of Jesus' miracles and teachings in each of the Gospels that contain them. The three synoptic Gospels contain most of the same material, while John contains miracles and teachings that the synoptics do not. In the case of the two events discussed in this lesson, the three synoptic Gospels cover them in sequential order: Matthew 12:1-8; 9-14; Mark 2:23-28; 3:1-6; Luke 6:1-5; 6-11. It is especially helpful, as in the case of this study guide, when reading a passage in Mark to read it also in Matthew and Luke (and John in the case of the feeding of the five thousand—the only miracle covered by all four Gospels). Mark being overall the shortest Gospel, the other accounts will usually add details that Mark doesn't cover.

Walking on Water

Mark 6:45-52

In this lesson we watch as Jesus miraculously walks across the water on the Sea of Galilee.

OUTLINE

Sometimes God puts us in difficult positions in order to test us. And believe it or not, many of Jesus' miracles involve this testing of faith. The miracle of Jesus walking on the water marks the second (not the first) time that Jesus used a storm on the Sea of Galilee to test His disciples.

I.   **The Pattern of the Test**

II. **The Preparation for the Test**
  A. Isolation
  B. Desperation

III. **The Process of the Test**
  A. What the Disciples Saw
  B. What the Disciples Said
  C. What the Disciples Felt
  D. What the Disciples Heard

IV. **The Purpose of the Test**
  A. The Wonder of Jesus
  B. The Worship of Jesus

V.   **The Promise for the Test**

The miracle of Jesus walking on the water is recorded for us in the Gospels of Matthew, Mark, and John; only Luke does not record it. In all three instances where this miracle is recorded, it always follows right after the feeding of the five thousand. You will see why as this study unfolds.

Before we look at these verses, please take note that this is a different storm from the one we already studied in Mark 4:35-41. That storm seemed to be almost demonic in character because Jesus rebuked the storm and it was instantly quelled. In this passage, the storm described is simply a reflection of the wind blowing in the wrong direction and the disciples having a hard time trying to get where they want to go.

In the first storm, Jesus is in the boat with the disciples (even though He is asleep). In the storm found here in Mark 6, Jesus is not in the boat. He actually ends up coming to the boat, but He is not in the boat during the storm. These are two different storms—but the same Jesus, the same disciples, and the same Sea of Galilee.

THE PATTERN OF THE TEST

There is a pattern for the test. In verse 45 we learn that "immediately He made His disciples get into the boat and go before Him to the other side, to Bethsaida, while He sent the multitude away." The reason we know the importance of connecting the feeding of the five thousand and Jesus' walking on the water during the storm is because John tells us in John 6:14-15:

> Then those men, when they had seen the sign that Jesus did, said, "This is truly the Prophet who is to come into the world." Therefore, when Jesus perceived that they were about to come and take Him by force to make Him king, He departed again to the mountain by Himself alone.

The crowd that had been there the day Jesus fed them was dangerously fueled with Messianic fever.[1] They saw what Jesus did and they wanted to make Him their king right then and there. Jesus realized what their intentions were and He didn't want that to happen because He knew His time had not come yet.

And so, the Bible says two things happened: Jesus made His disciples get into a boat and go to the other side of the sea, and Jesus went to the mountains to pray. The time of testing that we're going to examine with the disciples comes after a mountaintop experience. Remember that often the depth of the wave is equal to the height of the wave that goes before it.

Oftentimes, directly after a mountaintop experience, a valley will be encountered. We not only know that because the Scripture teaches it, we know it because it happens to us. When we have a moment of great victory in our lives, we are more vulnerable than we know. After the mountaintop, look out for the valley!

THE PREPARATION FOR THE TEST

In preparation for the test, verse 45 tells us that Jesus "made His disciples get into the boat and go before Him to the other side, to Bethsaida, while He sent the multitude away." Here is another lesson that God is impressing upon us. The Bible says that Jesus— watch carefully—made His disciples get into the boat and go to the other side.

Apparently that is not what they wanted to do, because the word used here has an intensity about it that conveys urgency. It is almost like Jesus forced them against their will to get into the boat. Maybe they just wanted to stay with Jesus, but He thrust them into this boat and sent them to the middle of the Sea of Galilee, right into the teeth of a terrible storm.

Jesus did that, and He did it to His very own disciples. Do you think He didn't know what was going to happen? Surely, He knew. Sometimes God engineers problems so that we can see how insufficient we are, leading us to then trust in Him for the sufficiency that only He alone can provide. This time of testing for the disciples was marked by two characteristics.

Isolation

First of all, the scene is lonely. Mark 6:47 describes it this way: "Now when evening came, the boat was in the middle of the sea; and He was alone on the land." Matthew 14:24-25 tells us, "But the boat was now in the middle of the sea, tossed by the waves, for the wind was contrary. Now in the fourth watch of the night Jesus went to them."

And John tells the story this way: "Now when evening came, His disciples went down to the sea, got into the boat, and went over the sea toward Capernaum. And it was already dark, and Jesus had not come to them" (John 6:16-17).

Reading these verses carefully, you can tell that this was an eerie time of night. The disciples had been sailing all night long and it was between three and six o'clock in the morning. They were in the middle of the Sea of Galilee, rowing their boat for all they were worth against the howling wind. It was a time of isolation.

Desperation

This was also a time of desperation. Note verse 48: "Then He saw them straining at rowing, for the wind was against them." John 6:18 tells us, "Then the sea arose because a great wind was blowing." The disciples had set out for Capernaum, but the more they rowed, the more the wind was blowing against them. They were rowing into the wind, and the wind was not helping them— the wind and the disciples were at cross purposes.

John 6:19 fills in some additional details: "So when they had rowed about three or four miles...." The total length of the journey that Jesus instructed them to take was about five miles. They had already rowed roughly three or four miles, so they were more than halfway there.

Remember that earlier Matthew said that Jesus came to them in the fourth watch of the night? Now consider this: They had begun their journey toward the evening hours, so the disciples had been rowing on the Sea of Galilee for somewhere between seven and nine hours!

It had taken them seven to nine hours to travel just three or four miles. You can begin to understand the magnitude of the winds they were facing. Essentially, they were treading water in the middle of the Sea of Galilee. They weren't going anywhere!

From Jesus' vantage point, "He saw them straining at rowing" (Mark 6:48). In other words, they were giving it everything they had. After seven to nine hours in that condition, they weren't even thinking about getting to Capernaum—they were desperately trying to save their lives. The wind was so strong, they didn't know if they were going to make it. But God had them right where He wanted them to be.

THE PROCESS OF THE TEST

The testing of Jesus' disciples involved four different experiences, which we can learn and apply to our personal walk with God.

What the Disciples Saw

What did the disciples see? Mark 6:48 tells us that Jesus "came to them, walking on the sea, and would have passed them by." As the disciples were rowing with all of their hearts, with weariness setting in from an all-nighter, they look up and see something moving across the top of the water toward them. John 6:19 tells us "they saw Jesus walking on the sea and drawing near the boat; and they were afraid."

In other words, Jesus was not only coming toward them, He was gaining on them! Just stop and think about that for a moment. The disciples saw a figure gliding across the top of the water, and He was going at such a speed that they thought He was going to go right past them. And when He got alongside them, Jesus looked at them and said, "It is I; do not be afraid" (John 6:20). That is what they saw and experienced!

What the Disciples Said

When the disciples first saw Jesus, "they supposed it was a ghost, and cried out" (Mark 6:49). The book of Matthew adds that "when the disciples saw Him walking on the sea, they were troubled, saying, 'It is a ghost!' And they cried out for fear" (Matthew 14:26).

The word for *ghost* in the New Testament language is the word *phantasm*, from which we get our word *phantom*. They thought what they saw was a phantom, a ghost. They couldn't comprehend that it was Jesus walking on the water toward them.

What the Disciples Felt

Verse 50 explains to us what they felt, "for they all saw Him and were troubled." Is that not the greatest understatement of Scripture? Matthew 14:26 says that "they cried out for fear," and John 6:19 makes it known that "they were afraid." In other words, panic was ricocheting throughout the boat. Some were standing, some were screaming, perhaps some were ready to jump into the sea.

Why were they so afraid? Let's face it, we would have been afraid, too. But once they saw that it was Jesus, why were they still afraid? Later in verse 52 we find the answer: "For they had not understood about the loaves, because their heart was hardened."

What had they not understood about the loaves? The disciples had still not figured out that Jesus was the Son of the Living God, and that He was personally involved with them.

They knew something miraculous had happened when fifteen thousand people were fed from a young boy's snack. But they still didn't connect the dots that the One who made that happen was the Messiah, the Son of God. Their hearts were hardened.

So when they were in the storm and Jesus appeared to them walking on the sea, they were still afraid because they did not understand. They lived with Jesus every day and they still didn't get it. And so, they reacted accordingly—with fear, not faith.

What the Disciples Heard

As the disciples quaked with fear, almost paralyzed, a voice pierced the storm: "Be of good cheer! It is I; do not be afraid" (verse 50). The disciples had not yet processed who the "I" in the "It is I" really was. But isn't that a great statement for all of us to hold on to? Whenever we are afraid, we just need to realize that Jesus is in our situation, telling us to be of good cheer.

THE PURPOSE OF THE TEST

What was the purpose of all of this? What was the purpose of the test? In verses 51 and 52, Scripture says that Jesus went up into the boat after He had identified Himself, and immediately the wind ceased. Let's consider all the things Jesus did in this moment.

The Wonder of Jesus

This incredible event detailed in the Word of God contains not just one, but four miracles. Two of them are seen in the book of Mark, one is found in Matthew, and the other miracle is detailed in John. They are all about the same event, and they all point to the wonder of Jesus.

1. Jesus Walked on the Water

The first wonder, of course, is when Jesus walked on the water. Verse 48 declares that they saw Jesus walking on the sea—miracle number one. Not only was Jesus able to walk on water, He was able to walk on water in the middle of a windstorm, no less.

2. Jesus Calmed the Sea

The Bible says in verse 51 that as soon as Jesus got inside the boat, the wind suddenly stopped and the storm was over. It didn't just slow down or quietly begin to recede; the storm stopped in an instant and the sea was calmed. This was miracle number two.

3. Peter Walked on the Water

The third miracle is not found in Mark's account, but it is detailed in Matthew's report. Peter, like Jesus, ended up walking on the water. There is a huge debate about why that story is not included in Mark's Gospel. Here is my explanation.

Mark's Gospel is really Peter's account of everything he experienced with Jesus, and Peter dictated it to Mark who wrote it down. So why would Peter tell this story and leave out his walking on the water in this account? He was embarrassed! While it took great faith to walk on the water, Matthew 14:30-31 tells us that Peter became "afraid; and beginning to sink he cried out, saying, 'Lord, save me!' And immediately Jesus stretched out His hand and caught him, and said to him, 'O you of little faith, why did you doubt?'"

Peter not only started sinking because of his lack of faith, but Jesus also reprimanded him. Would you want that included in the official record if you were Peter? I think not! Thankfully, Matthew saw fit to record this part of the story so that we have a full picture of what really happened that day.

4. They Were Transported Immediately to the Other Side

The last miracle might surprise you. It is found in John 6:21: "Then they willingly received Him into the boat, and immediately the boat was at the land where they were going."

How would you like to have been on that ride? Jesus got into the boat and immediately they were right at the shore! They were at least a couple of miles out from shore, but when Jesus got in the boat, He did away with that distance in the blink of an eye.

The Worship of Jesus

The wonder of Jesus eventuated into the worship of Jesus. Matthew 14:33 tells us, "Then those who were in the boat came and worshiped Him, saying, 'Truly You are the Son of God.'" They finally got it!

But look at what God had to do to get through to the hardened hearts of His disciples. He fed fifteen thousand people with a little boy's lunch. He walked on the water. He calmed the sea twice. He got Peter to walk on the water. He took them on the fastest boat trip recorded in history. And only after all that was done did they realize that Jesus was the Son of God.

THE PROMISE FOR THE TEST

Let's end by looking at the promise for this test. For a moment, make a split screen image in your mind. On the left, you see the disciples on their boat in the midst of the storm. On the right, you see Jesus up on the mountain—praying for them! As they were in the midst of the storm, Jesus was praying for His disciples.

When we go through our storms, even though the Lord often engineers them to test us, He never stops praying for us. The Bible tells us that Jesus is in heaven at this very moment interceding on our behalf. So be encouraged today to know that He sees you and He is praying for you. You may be going through a test, but Jesus isn't going to leave you without His help and encouragement. He is always praying for us through our storms.

Note

1. C. E. B. Cranfield, *The Gospel According to St. Mark* (Cambridge: Cambridge University Press, 1983), 175.

1. Read Mark 6:45-48.

   a. After everyone was fed, what two things did Jesus do? (verse 45)

   b. Once everyone was gone, where did Jesus go? To do what? (verse 46)

   c. Once darkness had fallen, where could the disciples be found? In the meantime, where was Jesus? (verse 47)

   d. What could Jesus see the disciples doing from His high vantage point? (verse 48)

e. What was causing the disciples their problems on the Sea of Galilee? (verse 48)

2. Read Mark 6:48-52.

   a. Later on that night, how did Jesus come to His disciples? (verse 48)

   b. Jesus was walking so fast that the Bible gives us what incredible detail at the end of verse 48?

   c. What did the disciples do when they saw Jesus? What did they think He was? (verse 49)

d. Seeing that they were troubled at the sight of Him, what did Jesus say to calm them down? (verse 50)

e. What happened when Jesus climbed into their boat? (verse 51)

f. What was the disciples' response to these miraculous acts? (verse 51)

g. In light of the feeding of the five thousand, why did they still lack understanding? (verse 52)

GROUP QUESTIONS

1. Read Matthew 14:22-33 and discuss the following questions.

   a. Peter was the only disciple who had enough faith to walk out to Jesus on the water, but when he succumbed to fear, Jesus reprimanded him for his lack of faith. Why do you think Jesus was hard on Peter but not on the others who dared not leave the boat?

   b. Matthew's account tells us that at Jesus' walking on the water, the disciples finally realized that Jesus was "the Son of God." Discuss reasons why the feeding of the five thousand was not enough for them to believe, but this act finally was.

c. Peter walked on the water with Jesus but ended up denying Him three times at His greatest time of trial. What should we learn from Peter's life and example? What should we be careful of?

2. Read Luke 6:12-16.

a. Jesus prayed all night on a mountain the day before He chose His twelve apostles. He often prayed in the hills around Galilee. Talk about why you think Jesus went in the mountains to pray at night. Is there anything we can learn from His example that we can implement into our own lives? Discuss.

b. Has there ever been a time when you spent all night in prayer? Why? What was it like?

DID YOU KNOW?

In 1986, an ancient boat was discovered buried in the mud on the shore of the Sea of Galilee. After many strenuous and strategic efforts to extract it without destroying it, this vessel was found to be dated back to 1 A.D., the time when Christ was alive. Now known as the "Jesus Boat," this piece of history can be seen today in a museum next to the Sea of Galilee. Though there are no known or verified identifications of this particular boat with Jesus and the disciples, it gives the viewer an incredible look and sense of the exact kind of vessel that they would have sailed on in their many journeys across the Sea of Galilee.

C'MON GET REAL

Mark 7:1-23

*In this lesson we observe as Jesus' words destroy the
false traditions and doctrines of the Pharisees.*

OUTLINE

From the time of Jesus until now, all religious people have set out to
create their own unwritten rules that end up dominating their lives. But
as you will see in this lesson, Jesus destroyed any notion of legalistic
purity. God's Word stands alone in authority, and any attempts to
add to it only reveal a heart with sinful and corrupt motives.

I. **The Accusation**

II. **The Confrontation**

III. **The Illustration**

IV. **The Application**
   A. His Words to the Multitude
   B. His Words to His Disciples

   Conclusion
   1. The Application to Christians
   2. The Application to Non-Christians

One does not have to be a sociologist or a marketing expert to understand that our culture has become infatuated with fitness, youth, beauty, and appearance. Billions of dollars are spent every year on cosmetic surgeries, exercise programs, fitness books, and diet programs. In fact, the television industry would go out of business if the infomercials for all these products were taken off the air. We are a people committed to the outward appearance of our lives.

In light of that, it is very interesting to stack up that vanity industry against God's perspective during the time when a king was being chosen for Israel. In 1 Samuel 16:7, God says, "Do not look at his appearance or at his physical stature, because I have refused him. For the Lord does not see as man sees; for man looks at the outward appearance, but the Lord looks at the heart."

From Samuel's day until ours, these two ideas about the meaning of life have continued to be in conflict with one another. And here in the seventh chapter of the book of Mark, we will examine one of the most violent collisions between these two ideologies found anywhere in the Bible.

Up until this point in Mark's Gospel, we have been examining the works of Jesus. But for just a few chapters in the center of the book, that gets turned upside down and we begin to hear Jesus' teaching. This is some of the most vibrant and important and visceral teaching of the Lord Jesus Christ you will find anywhere in the Gospels.

THE ACCUSATION

Here in this section, we have the most important words of Jesus in the book of Mark. This story begins in verse 5 with an accusation toward Jesus and the disciples: "Then the Pharisees and scribes asked Him, 'Why do Your disciples not walk according to the tradition of the elders, but eat bread with unwashed hands?'"

The Pharisees came to Jesus and His disciples loaded with ammunition. They have observed them eating with unwashed hands, which is better translated as "unrinsed hands" because this really wasn't about hygiene or cleanliness. This was about a ceremonial washing. They were not failing to practice cleanliness—they were failing to follow a tradition of ceremonially rinsing their hands before they ate.

Here is how they would do it: They would pour water over their hands, which was supposed to ceremonially cleanse them from anything that could defile them. It involved pouring water out of a jar on another's hands from the top of the jar. They would start by pouring it down over the top of their fingers until it ran off of their wrist; they would then turn it over and pour it down over their wrist until it ran off of their fingers. They would finish by dabbing it dry with their fist. This was the process to become ceremonially clean.

Please note that in verses 3 and 4 of the text that it says that the disciples were not in violation of the Law—they were in violation of the tradition of the elders. According to the Pharisees, when God gave the written law to Moses on Mount Sinai, He also gave an oral law to Moses. There is no record of that in the Bible and no evidence that it ever happened. Nevertheless, the Pharisees and the elders had recorded this oral law of God, and it was memorialized at the end of the second century A.D. in what is now referred to as the "Mishnah."[1]

In other words, the Law wasn't specific enough for the Pharisees. They had to have more information about how the Law was to work. The creation of the oral law, supposedly, defined the practical outworking of the Law. And over the years, the oral law began to grow more powerful than the written Law, becoming absolutely absurd in the process.

For example, the oral law prohibited a Jew from looking into the mirror on the Sabbath because he might see a gray hair and be tempted to pull it out; the act of pulling out that hair would be work and therefore would violate the Sabbath. So here we find the Pharisees accusing the followers of Jesus of not living up to the traditions of the elders.

THE CONFRONTATION

The accusation resulted in a confrontation that is recorded in verses 6 through 9:

He answered and said to them, "Well did Isaiah prophesy of you hypocrites, as it is written:

'This people honors Me with their lips,
But their heart is far from Me.

And in vain they worship Me,
Teaching as doctrines the commandments of men.'

For laying aside the commandment of God, you hold the tradition of men—the washing of pitchers and cups, and many other such things you do." He said to them, "All too well you reject the commandment of God, that you may keep your tradition."

Jesus began His confrontation with the Pharisees by quoting Isaiah 29:13. Nothing could have described the conduct of these men any better than the words of their own revered prophet, Isaiah. Using Isaiah's words, Jesus told the Pharisees that they were phonies and hypocrites. They were acting out something that was not representing their hearts. Their religion had become mechanical and thoughtless. Their lips and their hearts were far apart. They were not real.

When you read what the Pharisees were doing, you want to say to them, "C'mon, get real!" They had allowed their traditions to grow up and replace the Word of God in their lives. But Jesus was willing to confront them with this most pressing issue of religion.

Any time you try to put your own opinion or your own ideas on the same level with the authority of the Word of God, you are trafficking in dangerous territory. In the early transition period between Judaism and Christianity, the elders began to elevate the Mishnah above the Torah, and it was the beginning of the breakdown of Judaism. And it still has its tentacles reaching out to this day.

THE ILLUSTRATION

If you ever have studied the teaching of Jesus, you will discover that one aspect of His preaching is that it can be frightening and wonderful all at the same time. He makes His words so plain that you can't avoid their truth. He will paint you into a corner with His truth and you won't be able to get out. That is what He is about to do with these Pharisees.

Having already accused the Pharisees of being phonies and hypocrites when it comes to their observance of the Law, Jesus then gave them an illustration so they would not misunderstand His words. The picture He painted was clear, colorful, and irrefutable.

The first thing Jesus did was remind them of a section of the Law recorded in Exodus 20:12, also referred to again in Exodus 21:17. Here is what the Law says: "Honor your father and your mother, that your days may be long upon the land which the Lord your God is giving you . . . And he who curses his father or his mother shall surely be put to death."

Now when we usually read those words, we think about little children being obedient to their parents. But this Law is not talking about little children being obedient to their parents; it is talking about adult children taking care of their parents.

Within their oral law, the Pharisees had come up with a plan called "Corban," a word that means "dedicated to God." It ultimately came to mean "untouchable." This is what it was: You could take your money and your assets and place them in a trust fund called "Corban." It was a trust fund supposedly dedicated to God that could not be used for anything else.

So when young adult Jews realized how much money it was going to cost them to care for their parents, they would take all of their assets and put them into Corban, therefore alleviating them of the responsibility to care for their parents. They were using the oral tradition of the elders to escape the impact of the Law!

But they sat there that day trembling in their boots because Jesus nailed them with His illustration. They were hypocrites and they were substituting outer ritual for inner reality. They drew near to God with their lips, but their hearts were far from Him.

And according to Jesus, the violation of the Corban rule was not an isolated infraction, because He said at the end, "And many other such things you do." They were always trying to skirt the nature of the Law by coming up with their own oral traditions that would nullify it.

THE APPLICATION

Jesus' application for this teaching is divided into two sections.

His Words to the Multitude

First of all, Jesus speaks to the multitude in verses 14-16: "Hear Me, everyone, and understand: There is nothing that enters a man from outside which can defile him; but the things which come out of him, those are the things that defile a man. If anyone has ears to hear, let him hear!"

In these words, Jesus redefines the fundamental concept of clean and unclean for everybody—especially for the devastated Pharisees. Rinsing your hands ceremonially has no effect at all on your heart.[2] Uncleanness and defilement and separation from God are all matters of the intention of the heart, not the violation of cultural rituals and formalities.

His Words to His Disciples

Jesus is then going to get even more specific. In verse 17 we find "when He had entered a house away from the crowd, His disciples asked Him concerning the parable." Jesus must have been very discouraged. He taught them as no man ever taught—He was the greatest Teacher in the world—and they still did not get it.

Jesus responded by saying in verse 18, "Do you not perceive that whatever enters a man from outside cannot defile him, because it does not enter his heart but his stomach, and is eliminated, thus purifying all foods?" That one little statement got Jesus nailed to the cross. That one little statement declared war on the Pharisees and their superficial righteousness.

Defilement comes from within—that is where the problem lies. It is not the washing of your hands or your utensils—any outward display—that corrupts. It is your heart! It comes from inside.

Jesus then went one step further and listed all the evil things that come from within: "out of the heart of men, proceed evil thoughts, adulteries, fornications, murders, thefts, covetousness, wickedness, deceit, lewdness, an evil eye, blasphemy, pride, foolishness." The Pharisees were worried about whether their pots and pans were clean, and Jesus said, "No, here are your problems."

Jesus lists thirteen sins of the heart. The first seven are plural, denoting evil acts, and the last six are singular, denoting evil attitudes. Sin affects us all, and we all know it. Romans 3:10 says, "There is none righteous; no, not one." We have all gone astray—every single one of us.

The cancer of sin has affected every part of mankind. We all have the disease, and it has affected us in every part of our lives. And whether we like it or not, this is the truth.

CONCLUSION

So what does this passage from the book of Mark mean to all of us living today? There is one grand principle that can be applied in two ways.

The Application to Christians

If you are already a follower of Christ, these words have a special meaning for you. There is a theological term called *sanctification* that refers to an inside-out process. For a Christian, sanctification means becoming in practice what you already are in perfection. The Bible says that in Jesus Christ you are clean and whole and righteous.

And sanctification is the process of becoming more and more like Him in the way that you live.

Quit worrying so much about what people think, and begin to care more about what God thinks. God sees the heart—man sees the outside. We are Christians outwardly, but often we are not Christians inwardly. Until we get real with our faith and quit playing the game and posturing for other people instead of asking God what He wants from us, we won't grow in our faith or in holiness.

The Application to Non-Christians

If you are not a Christian, there is some good news inserted for you: While sanctification is an inside-out process, salvation is also an inside-out process. God has provided a plan to fix your heart. He wants to give you a heart transplant—a spiritual heart transplant. Ezekiel 36:26 says, "I will give you a new heart and put a new spirit within you; I will take the heart of stone out of your flesh and give you a heart of flesh."

The Bible says if we open our heart and receive Jesus Christ, He will come and live within us and He will clean us up from the inside out. When we put our trust in Him, He takes away our sin and replaces it with His righteousness.

You can't do that from the outside in. You have to do that from the inside out. To be a Christian, you need a new heart. And I want to tell you that Jesus Christ is in the new heart business.

Notes

1. Herbert Danby, trans, *The Mishnah* (London: Oxford University Press, 1974), 452.

2. Michael Card, *Mark—The Gospel of Passion* (Downers Grove, IL: InterVarsity Press, 1957), 99.

3. R. Kent Hughes, *Mark, Volume 1: Jesus, Servant and Savior* (Wheaton, IL: Crossway Books, 1989), 163.

1. Read Mark 7:1-13.

   a. What two groups came to accuse Jesus and the disciples? (verse 1)

   b. Where did they come from? (verse 1)

   c. In your own words, paraphrase the issue that the Pharisees had with Jesus and the disciples. (verses 2-5)

d. In verses 6-7, Jesus marks the Pharisees' hypocrisy by saying their lips only pretend to honor the Lord. What three things does Jesus say are true of them?

e. The Pharisees were putting their own traditions above what? (verse 8)

f. In verse 9, Jesus says that they openly reject God's commandments so that they can do what?

g. Catching them in a bind, in verse 13 Jesus makes what shocking statement concerning the Pharisees' actions?

GROUP QUESTIONS

1. Read Matthew 23:23-24 and discuss the following questions.

   a. Jesus said the Pharisees were careful to pay their tithes but neglected to fight for what three major issues? (verse 23)

   b. Explain why the analogy involving the gnat and the camel in verse 24 is so appropriate to Jesus' point in verse 23. List and discuss some blind guides in modern culture who also completely miss the point.

2. Read Matthew 23:25-28.

   a. Jesus employs a metaphor of the Pharisees cleaning the outside of the cup while the inside is still filthy. Discuss other examples of having a clean outside and a dirty inside that apply to this teaching.

   b. Jesus said that the Pharisees appeared righteous, but in actuality could be marked by what two traits? (verse 28)

   c. The image of white-washed tombs full of the dead is quite striking. Are there any white-washed tombs in your own life that you are fooling yourself about?

3. Read Luke 6:43-45.

   a. What is the clearest indication of the condition of a man's
      heart? (verse 45) By this measure, how would you gauge the
      quality of your fruit?

DID YOU KNOW?

The Mishnah is a collection of the supposed oral laws of Moses and of God. According to the Pharisaical tradition, the Mishnah was given to build a fence around the law. R. Kent Hughes gives us an example of the ridiculous nature of these laws: "According to the Mishnah, you could not carry a handkerchief on the Sabbath. You could wear one but you could not carry one. So if you were upstairs and wanted to take your handkerchief downstairs, you would have to tie it around your neck, walk downstairs and untie it. Then you could blow your nose."[3] Jesus saw this as the absolute nonsense that it was and bravely called it out as such!

WHAT HAPPENS IN CHURCH STAYS IN CHURCH

Mark 7:24-37

In this lesson we watch as Jesus dramatically heals two non-Jewish people by unusual means.

OUTLINE

It is often taken for granted that the salvation Jesus affords to those who trust in Him is for both the Gentile and the Jew. However, before He came and knocked down those barriers, the Gentiles were on the outside looking in. But praise God that Jesus had the power to heal, and that He revealed Himself to everyone—declaring that all people could find hope in His Name.

I. **Reaching Beyond Our Cultural Zone**
    A. The Place Where Jesus Went
    B. The Person Jesus Met
    C. The Prayer Jesus Heard
    D. The Parable Jesus Told
    E. The Promise Jesus Made

II. **Reaching Beyond Our Comfort Zone**
    A. The Impossible Problem
    B. The Impassioned Plea
    C. The Improbable Procedure
    D. The Incredible Power
    E. The Intriguing Prohibition
    F. The Irrefutable Proof

OVERVIEW

You have heard and seen the phrase many times, "What happens in Vegas, Stays in Vegas." Whenever anybody says that, what they really mean is they are planning to do something in Las Vegas that they hope nobody finds out about back home.

I want to take that sinful and secular way of thinking, stand it on its head, and use it for another purpose. Are we guilty of this—not having what we have learned and experienced at church affect our lives? We come to the sanctuary and we enact our liturgical rituals, and then we go back home to our work and our lives. And whatever took place in church stays in church and does not affect anything we do during the week. So in effect, what happens in church, stays in church.

That is obviously not God's intention or purpose for the Church that He established. But the "what happens in church, stays in church" mentality was the way Judaism openly operated until Jesus came to disrupt it. The Jews believed that they owned a corner on the market of God, that He was their own special God and was not available to anybody else.

In fact, they did not consider anyone else worthy of their God. They referred to the Gentiles as dogs! But Jesus is about to change that in these two accounts found in Mark 7. Jesus understood that the Gospel did come first to the Jews. But there was also a plan for the Gospel to go to the Gentiles.

So while the Jews held tightly to their rituals and their restrictions, Jesus stood in the midst of them all, wanting to expand the message of hope that was found in Himself, the Messiah, to all people. And so, we find the Lord Jesus leaving Galilee and the comfort of the Jewish territory, and going to a Gentile region outside of Israel.

By traveling to Tyre and Sidon, Jesus made a historic statement that the Gospel was not only for the Jews but also for the Gentiles. Once He left His cultural zone and went into the Gentile lands, He performed two miracles that are the core of this study. These two miracles are done for a specific purpose—to demonstrate that the Gospel of Jesus Christ is for the entire world.

REACHING BEYOND OUR CULTURAL ZONE

As we begin this study with Jesus reaching beyond our cultural zone, it is interesting to note that the elements of the story are arranged in such a way as to provide an illustration of the perfect examples of people who are both outside of Jesus' cultural zone and outside of the Jewish cultural zone. He couldn't have picked more perfect specimens for His illustration.

The Place Where Jesus Went

Verse 24 tells us that Jesus "went to the region of Tyre and Sidon. And He entered a house and wanted no one to know it, but He could not be hidden." Jesus left Galilee and has journeyed about twenty miles into an area called Tyre and Sidon, which is modern Lebanon today. Even though this is Gentile country, Jesus' ministry preceded Him and people everywhere knew who He was. Any attempts at anonymity for Him were futile, even in this far country.

The miracles that Jesus performed here were at the most unlikely place you could imagine, for Tyre and Sidon was the homeland of Jezebel. Jezebel, the wife of Ahab, was the queen who tried to bring idolatry into Israel and mingle it together with Judaism. She almost destroyed the kingdom of Israel by her wicked heart and her association with the prophets of Baal. It is into this place that Jesus goes.

The Person Jesus Met

Let's now look at the person that Jesus met. Verses 25 and 26 say, "For a woman whose young daughter had an unclean spirit heard about Him, and she came and fell at His feet. The woman was a Greek, a Syro-Phoenician by birth." In Matthew's account of this story, he adds that this was a woman of Canaan, a place that was despicable to the Jewish people. She was the most unlikely candidate for salvation you could ever imagine.

Everything you can think of was against this woman. Her nationality was against her: She was a Gentile; Jesus was a Jew. Her gender was against her: She was a woman, and in that particular time, men dominated the landscape. And even Satan was against her because she had come to ask Jesus to cast a demon out of her daughter.[1]

And as you read the story, you are almost made to believe that perhaps Jesus was against her, because when she comes and begs

Jesus to heal her little daughter, He tells her a story that on the surface doesn't quite make sense. But Jesus knew what He was doing.

The Prayer Jesus Heard

The prayer that Jesus heard was a prayer of intense passion. Matthew 15:22 tells us that she prayed so much that she cried out, "Have mercy on me, O Lord, Son of David!" She didn't even know what that meant! Perhaps she had heard other people say it, but she was pleading over and over again for Jesus to help her stricken daughter.

The Bible tells us the disciples got irritated about it. Matthew tells us that she pleaded so much that the disciples finally came to Jesus in Matthew 15:23 and asked Him to get rid of her because she was driving them crazy. She was very intense in her passion for the healing of her daughter, and did not care what anyone else thought about it. No doubt she had tried everything she knew to do in order that this demon might be taken away from her daughter, and nothing had worked.

So, she came because she had heard that Jesus had cast demons out of people. She did not care what was right or culturally proper or whether people believed she was a nuisance. She loved her daughter and she was going to do whatever it took to help her daughter. She would break down every barrier that was there just to get an audience with the Savior.

The Parable Jesus Told

Jesus responded to this woman in a rather strange way. In verse 27, He said to her, "Let the children be filled first, for it is not good to take the children's bread and throw it to the little dogs." This woman is begging Jesus for her daughter's safety and sanity, and Jesus tells her this parable! But let's look at what the parable means.

In Jesus' example, the children represent the Jews, the children's bread represents the mercy of God, and the little dogs represent the Gentiles. Jesus used the little puppies under the table to illustrate His presentation that the Jews were first in God's priority program, but there was also a place for the Gentiles, too. He was sent first to the lost sheep of Israel, but afterward the Gospel was going to be for all other nations.[2]

It is really interesting to note that as you read the parable, the woman was not angry at Jesus' response. She took it all in stride. Here is what she understood—there is enough grace in one little breadcrumb from Jesus to fix every problem in your life. She wasn't going to clamor for the priority that the Jews held in the Gospel; she was just happy to get in on the overflow of that into her life.

Listen to her answer in verse 28: "Yes, Lord, yet even the little dogs under the table eat from the children's crumbs." This woman understood what Jesus was saying. She knew she did not deserve to be fed at the table. She realized that His main purpose in coming was to fulfill the prophecies of the Jewish prophets concerning their coming Messiah, that He had come to the Jews first. She was merely determined to receive some crumbs.

The Promise Jesus Made

At that moment, Jesus made a promise to her in verses 29 and 30: "For this saying go your way; the demon has gone out of your daughter." Matthew 15:28 adds that Jesus said, "O woman, great is your faith! Let it be to you as you desire." Jesus recognized so much faith in this woman's acceptance of God's plan and priority that He healed her little girl.

REACHING BEYOND OUR COMFORT ZONE

Next, we come to the second story that involves someone else needing healing. The first story helps us understand how we can reach beyond our cultural zone. God reached down and touched the life of a Gentile woman in a heathen land. Now we are going to see a story about Jesus reaching beyond our comfort zone.

The Impossible Problem

Walking through the Decapolis region, verse 32 tells us, "Then they brought to Him one who was deaf and had an impediment in his speech." Jesus had been to the Decapolis before, for it was there He met a man who had a legion of demons that He subsequently cast into a herd of swine, who ran down the slope into the water and were drowned. How do you think this man knew that Jesus had the power to heal? He heard about it from the man restored from the legion.

The Bible says that this new man who encountered Jesus had a hearing problem and a speech impediment, which tells us that he wasn't born that way. His problem wasn't that he couldn't speak; his problem was that his speech had an impediment in it. Somewhere along the way in this young man's life, something traumatic had happened to him that had caused him to lose his hearing. And in losing his hearing, he no longer had the ability to hear his speech, which in turn became jumbled.

In our culture today, we have many ways that we can deal with that problem with the use of hearing aids and speech therapists. But this man had nothing. He couldn't hear, and he was losing his ability to speak.

In that culture, such a man was more reprehensible than a person who was blind, for he would make squawking noises and sounds that were irritating. He would be the brunt of jokes, and the people around him would not want to be near him. He was considered to be obnoxious. He was a man who was outside of their comfort zone.

The Impassioned Plea

The Bible tells us that the people came to Jesus, and in verse 32, "they begged Him to put His hand on him." All they felt that man needed was a touch from the Master, so they came to Him in faith and uttered their plea before Him.

The Improbable Procedure

Jesus' response to their plea is remarkable, because heretofore in the book of Mark or in all the other Gospels, there is nothing like what Jesus is about to do. One takeaway from this is that Jesus is never to be stereotyped. He does His work in a lot of different ways. He tailors His ministry specifically to the people that He is ministering to. This healing is marked by three characteristics.

1. Isolation

The first thing Jesus does as He deals with this man is He takes him into isolation. Verse 33 says, "And He took him aside from the multitude." Jesus took the man out of the crowd and went to a solitary place because He doesn't want this man to face any more embarrassment. Jesus doesn't want to make a spectacle out of him—He just wants to help this hurting individual without any distractions in the way.

2. Identification

Secondly, Jesus "put His fingers in his ears, and He spat and touched his tongue." While on the earth, Jesus was a man who touched people. And when Jesus touched you, everything changed.

In this case, Jesus used a very special and unique procedure for this man who could not hear. If Jesus had said anything to him, it would have been useless, because that man wouldn't have heard it!

So Jesus took His two fingers and touched the man's ears as if to say in sign language, "I'm going to fix this." And then the Bible says He put some saliva on His finger and touched the man's tongue, signifying that He was going to fix that, too. Finally, the Bible says Jesus looked up to heaven, so the man would know from whence comes his healing.

3. Intercession

Thirdly, Jesus interceded for the man. Verse 34 says, "Then, looking up to heaven, He sighed, and said to him, 'Ephphatha,' that is, 'Be opened.'" That was the first word that man had heard in years. When Jesus said, "Ephphatha," that man's ears were opened, and he was instantaneously healed.

The Incredible Power

Verse 35 describes the results of Jesus' incredible power: "Immediately his ears were opened, and the impediment of his tongue was loosed, and he spoke plainly." In the Greek language it describes the loosing of his tongue; the phrase used literally means "and his tongue was unchained." The chains fell off his tongue, and he was able to speak clearly. He was immediately, completely restored. And everybody saw it!

The Intriguing Prohibition

But Jesus makes a curious statement after the healing in verse 36: "Then He commanded them that they should tell no one; but the more He commanded them, the more widely they proclaimed it." Jesus went into Decapolis twice and did two miracles. The first miracle time, He cast out demons and told the freed man to tell everyone. The second time, He healed a man's hearing and his speech and then told him to tell no one.

Why do you suppose Jesus did that? Because every single situation with Jesus was different. His message never changed, but His methods always changed. He wasn't a stereotyped person, and neither should we be. There's one message that's right for everyone, but there isn't one method that's right for everyone. The Gospel of Jesus Christ can be shared in many different ways.

The Irrefutable Proof

Verse 37 says the result of this miracle was that "they were astonished beyond measure, saying, 'He has done all things well. He makes both the deaf to hear and the mute to speak.'" Isn't that true? We serve a good God. He does all things well!

The same God who reached down and touched this man and that woman's daughter in a miraculous way wants to reach down and touch the hearts of men and women in our culture today. But we need to get comfortable living outside of our cultural zone and outside of our comfort zone. The people we meet today are candidates for the Gospel of Jesus Christ, and we must put them all back up on our radar screens and say, "God has called us to this place for such a time as this." Hallelujah!

Notes

1. Warren Wiersbe, *Mark: Be Diligent* (Colorado Springs: David C. Cook, 1987), 92.

2. Tim Keller, *King's Cross: The Story of the World in the Life of Jesus* (New York: Penguin Group, 2011), 85.

1. Read Mark 7:24-30.

   a. What did Jesus endeavor to do in verse 24?

   b. What happened that did not allow Him to be hidden? (verse 25)

   c. Why had this woman come to Jesus? (verse 25)

   d. What is remarkable about this woman's ethnic makeup? (verse 26)

   e. This woman would not stop pleading for Jesus to do what? (verse 26)

f. Jesus likened performing this miracle for her to what? (verse 27)

g. What was her response to Jesus' remark? (verse 28)

h. Because of the faith and boldness of her reply, what happened? (verses 29-30)

2. Read Mark 7:31-36.

   a. What area had Jesus returned to? (verse 31) What earlier miracle did He perform in this same vicinity?

b. What two things were wrong with the man that was brought to Jesus? (verse 32)

c. What simple things were they asking for Jesus to do for the man? (verse 32)

d. List all the steps in order of what Jesus did to heal this man. (verses 33-34)

e. At Jesus' word, what three incredible things happened? (verse 35)

f. What did Jesus tell them to do in the aftermath? What happened instead? (verse 36)

1. The testimony of Mark 7:37 is that Jesus "has done all things well." Talk about all the good things that Jesus has done for you in such marvelous ways. List the three most significant ones from your life experience below.

2. Read Acts 13:42-49 and discuss the following questions.

   a. What were the Gentiles begging for in verse 42?

   b. In contrast, what were the Jews doing in verse 45?

   c. What amazing, world-changing message did Paul and Barnabas give in verses 46 and 47?

d. What was the Gentile response to this word? (verse 48)

e. How has this world changed and affected your life? Are you as grateful as the Gentiles were in this passage of that good news?

3. Read Ephesians 3:1-7.

   a. What mystery was made known to Paul that was not made known to others?

   b. Why did Paul become a minister? What was his message?

c. Do we take for granted the age we live in and the grace we have received? Discuss.

DID YOU KNOW?

It is remarkable to go through the book of Mark and just look at all the times that Jesus literally touched people. Jesus took Peter's mother-in-law by the hand and lifted her up (1:3). He stretched out His hand and touched a leper to heal him (1:41). On the Sabbath day, Jesus told a man to stretch out his withered hand, and when Jesus touched him, he was healed (3:5). Jesus also took the hand of the twelve-year-old daughter of the ruler of the synagogue, and He raised her up out of death (4:41). We don't serve a distant God. We serve a God who walked amongst His people, who physically touched them, who loved them at their point of need.

HOW MANY MIRACLES DOES IT TAKE?

Mark 8:1-21

In this lesson we witness Jesus perform another miracle, only to find that His disciples are still without understanding.

OUTLINE

Sometimes people get caught up in learning new things, especially when it comes to aspects of their Christian faith and walk. They think that some new revelation is going to change their life. But in reality, the real problem is not found in learning what is not known, it is remembering that which we have forgotten.

I. **The Problem of Insufficient Meals**
   A. The Commitment of Jesus' Followers
   B. The Compassion of Jesus' Heart

II. **The Problem of Inadequate Memories**

III. **The Problem of an Inappropriate Message**

IV. **The Problem of an Incredible Misunderstanding**
   A. Jesus' Illustration
   B. Jesus' Indignation

The particular story we are about to analyze in Mark 8 fits into context with many of the past lessons we have studied. In fact, if you look closely, you will see that the theme throughout these stories is bread!

In Mark 6:41, we read of the Lord Jesus feeding five thousand men with the little loaves of bread that were presented. Later on, the disciples and Jesus were castigated by the Pharisees for not washing their hands before they ate their bread (Mark 7:5). And then we just learned about the woman who begged Jesus to cast the demon out of her daughter. His initial response to her included a parable about children's bread falling from the table (Mark 7:27-28).

In this lesson, we are going to learn about another miracle that Jesus performed, where He fed four thousand men with, once again, bread (Mark 8:4). After that event, the Lord Jesus has a major discussion with His disciples about the true meaning of bread (Mark 8:17). This whole section of Scripture is about bread! And the Lord Jesus Christ is saying to us as we study this book, "I am the bread of life. He who comes to Me shall never hunger" (John 6:35).

THE PROBLEM OF INSUFFICIENT MEALS

In this story found in Mark 8, we find an interesting interaction between the insufficiency of man and the sufficiency of God.

The Commitment of Jesus' Followers

Notice verse 1: "In those days, the multitude being very great and having nothing to eat, Jesus called His disciples to Him." Consider that thought for a moment. Here are thousands of people listening to Jesus teach. They listened to Him for three days, and they had run out of food. Perhaps they had brought food with them at the beginning, but after three days they had already eaten it all up. They were incredibly hungry.

Food has such an incredible impact on our lives. And so you have to admire these followers of Jesus. In fact, the Scripture uses a word to describe their connectedness to the Lord. It is a strong word in the Greek language that means to really be adhered to someone, to follow that person eagerly, to hang onto their every word in many respects.

At times, our commitment to Jesus leads us into the discomfort of saying "No" to some of the things we want to do. And in this situation, that is what happened.

The Compassion of Jesus' Heart

But along with the commitment of Jesus' followers is the compassion of Jesus' heart. We read in this context that Jesus said, "I have compassion on the multitude, because they have now continued with Me three days and have nothing to eat. And if I send them away hungry to their own houses, they will faint on the way; for some of them have come from afar" (verses 2-3).

Now just stop and consider for a moment that Jesus is the living Son of God. He is the second Person in the Holy Trinity, yet He is attentive to the fact that those who are listening to Him teach are hungry. He realized they would have to go away to their own homes without any food. And the Bible says He had compassion on them.

The "compassion" mentioned in the New Testament really means "innards"—that is, Jesus had a gut concern for them. In the very inward part of His life, He was deeply touched by the hunger of these people. It wasn't just a passing concern; it was a deep-seated, involved concern on the part of Jesus. And so, He calls His disciples together.

THE PROBLEM OF INADEQUATE MEMORIES

One thing that is absolutely certain in this next section of Scripture is that memory is the issue. Either Mark, in his writing of the book, forgot the first miracle that Jesus did just a few verses earlier and recorded it again with different information, or Jesus actually did two separate miracles and the disciples forgot. Which is it?

I'm sure you know what the answer to that is, but so that you never forget it, we are going to closely examine what happened. Let me resolve the issue for you by showing you the differences between the two miracles. There are at least nine differences between these two miracles!

First of all, there is a different period of time involved. The five thousand who were fed by Jesus were with Him for only one day, but the four thousand who were fed by Him were with Him for three whole days.

The people themselves were also different. The feeding of the five thousand involved predominantly Jews, but the feeding of the four thousand involved mostly Gentiles. And the locations were not the same. Jesus fed the five thousand in Galilee near Bethsaida; the feeding of the four thousand took place somewhere in Decapolis.

There are different procedures between the two miracles. In the feeding of the five thousand, Jesus said to His disciples, "You give them something to eat" (Mark 6:37). But in the feeding of the four thousand, Jesus simply asked in verse 5, "How many loaves do you have?" It is getting difficult to claim that this is the same miracle told twice.

But there are even more differences! In the feeding of the five thousand, the crowd is instructed to sit down. But in the feeding of the four thousand, there is no mention of the green grassy hills of Galilee. And Jesus offered different prayers! In the feeding of the thousand, Jesus offered a general prayer for both the bread and the fish, but in the feeding of the four thousand, He offered a specific prayer for the bread and another specific prayer for the fish.

There were different portions and provisions involved as well. In the first miracle, there were five loaves and two fish, and in the cleanup, there were twelve baskets full of fragments left over. But in the second miracle, there were seven loaves and a few small fish, and that cleanup resulted in seven large baskets full of fragments left over.

Even the baskets that they collected the leftovers in were different! In the feeding of the five thousand, the twelve baskets collected are designated by the Greek word kophinos, which means a small wicker basket—something you would carry your lunch in to work. But in the feeding of the four thousand, the seven baskets collected were exceptionally large. The word there is the word spuris, and it is a basket big enough to hold a man. This is the same type of basket that they let the apostle Paul down over a wall in as detailed in the book of Acts.

But if none of these facts convince you, just consider the words of Jesus in verses 19 and 20:

"When I broke the five loaves for the five thousand, how many baskets full of fragments did you take up?" They said to Him, "Twelve." "Also, when I broke the seven for the four thousand, how many large baskets full of fragments did you take up?" And they said, "Seven."

Yes, the miracles are similar, but as you can see, they are not the same! There is a memory problem in this passage, but it is not Mark's memory—it is the disciples' memory. They didn't get it the first time. And as you're sadly going to see, they didn't even get it the second time.

The Problem of an Inappropriate Message

After this second miracle of feeding a large crowd was concluded, "then the Pharisees came out and began to dispute with Him, seeking from Him a sign from heaven, testing Him. But He sighed deeply in His spirit, and said, 'Why does this generation seek a sign? Assuredly, I say to you, no sign shall be given to this generation'" (verses 11-12).

The Bible says that after the feeding of the multitude, they got back in the boat and sailed to a place called Dalmanutha. This was in the region of Magdala where Mary Magdalene was from, on the other side of the Sea of Galilee. At their arrival, a group of Pharisees was waiting for Jesus, demanding their own private Pharisaical demonstration of the glory and power of God.

But the Pharisees did not want just some normal earthly miracle. For in the book of John, chapter 6, verses 30-31 in another account of a similar situation, we read:

Therefore they said to Him, "What sign will You perform then, that we may see it and believe You? What work will You do? Our fathers ate the manna in the desert; as it is written, 'He gave them bread from heaven to eat.'"

Apparently, they wanted Jesus to give them a bread shower or do something that would be beyond anything they had ever seen. Only at this would they believe in Jesus. But verse 12 tells us that instead of receiving a sign from Jesus, they got a sigh from Jesus, saying, "Why does this generation seek a sign? Assuredly, I say to you, no sign shall be given to this generation."

And the Bible says in verse 13 that at that moment Jesus turned on His heel, "and He left them, and getting into the boat again, departed to the other side." Don't ever let that happen in your life. If the Spirit of God speaks to your heart about your relationship with Almighty God, don't walk away from it. It is one thing for you to walk away from God; it is another thing for the Lord to walk away from you. Don't let that happen. How solemn this moment was in the life of these Pharisees!

The Problem of an Incredible Misunderstanding

We have seen the problem of insufficiency in the meals, the problem of inadequate memory—they couldn't remember what

Jesus had done!—and an inappropriate message. But the real crux of the passage and the thing that broke the heart of the Lord was the problem of an incredible misunderstanding. Note verses 14-16:

> Now the disciples had forgotten to take bread, and they did not have more than one loaf with them in the boat. Then He charged them, saying, "Take heed, beware of the leaven of the Pharisees and the leaven of Herod." And they reasoned among themselves, saying, "It is because we have no bread."

Let's examine this situation from Jesus' perspective.

Jesus' Illustration

Recall that in the first miracle of the 5,000, we are told in the text that it was 5,000 men, so including women and children it was at least 15,000 people fed, most likely more around 20,000. And in the Mark illustration, there were 4,000 men, so with women and children it was probably around 16,000 people fed. So in those two miracles alone Jesus fed 36,000 people with two small lunches.

Now we find Jesus is in a boat with His disciples and they are upset because they only brought one loaf of bread, and they're afraid they are going to run out of food! And Jesus is incredulous—in our vernacular He would say, "Come on guys!"

That is exactly what happened. They got in the boat and then remembered they forgot their bread, and they only had one loaf for all of them to eat. But they are also in a boat with somebody who has just fed 36,000 people with His miraculous power. It is no wonder why Jesus was frustrated with His followers.

Jesus' Indignation

What happens as a result of that gross ignorance and stupidity is a spirit of indignation from our Lord. In fact, there are only two places in the New Testament where there is more frustration expressed on the part of the Lord Jesus. One was in the Garden of Gethsemane when He asked His disciples to pray with Him and they all fell asleep. Remember that? The other is when Peter told Jesus He couldn't go to the cross, and Jesus got very angry with Peter.

But apart from those two events, this is the most frustration to ever be recorded out of the lips of Jesus. And it was because of the incredible misunderstanding and unbelief in the hearts of His very own disciples. Even though Jesus' disciples loved Him and considered Him to be their leader, they did not even know who He was.

Later in the passage, Jesus said to them, "Who do men say that I am?" He then personally asked them, "Who do you say that I am?" We know from studying the New Testament that it wasn't until after the Resurrection of Jesus Christ that some of His disciples actually realized that they had been the disciples of the living Son of God for those three years. Their ignorance is evident here in this passage.

Let me ask you this question: If you are in a boat with the Son of God, are you going to worry about the fact that you've only got one loaf of bread? No—especially if He had just fed 36,000 people with mere scraps of food.

But they just didn't get it. And Jesus was so broken over the hardness of their hearts that He asks them one question after another. He literally asks them nine different questions, finishing with the most haunting one of all: "How is it you do not understand?"

Jesus has never done more to demonstrate His deity. He has never done more to show who He is than in what He has done before these men. They witnessed an incredible outpouring of abundance, mercy, grace, and compassion on the part of this Man. They saw His incredible miracle-working power, and they still do not fully understand who He is.

So the lesson for us is simple—we need to remember what God has done. We can't rejoice in what we don't remember.

We need to rejoice in what God has done. With God, there is always enough. No matter what we need, God has plenty of it, for the whole earth belongs to Him. Everything that you need belongs to God. He is enough. There's nothing we can ask of Him that He cannot do. He is an abundant God. Hallelujah!

1. Read Mark 8:1-10.

   a. What problem surfaces once again in verse 1?

   b. For what reasons does Jesus say He specifically has compassion on this group of people? (verse 2)

   c. What does Jesus say would happen if they weren't sent away as they were? (verse 3)

   d. What was the disciples' excuse for non-action? (verse 4)

   e. What food supplies were available? (verse 5)

f. Jesus was always careful to do what before He distributed the food? (verses 6-7)

g. After all were fed, where (be detailed) were the leftovers placed? (verse 8)

h. After the crowd ate, what did Jesus do with them? (verse 9)

i. What did Jesus do with the disciples after the miraculous meal? (verse 10)

2. Read Mark 8:11-21.

   a. What were the two true intents of the Pharisees as they sought out Jesus? (verse 11)

b. How does Jesus reply and diffuse their intents? (verse 12)

c. In the midst of the confrontation with the Pharisees, what had the disciples forgotten? (verse 14)

d. What does Jesus warn the disciples about? (verse 15)

e. What do the disciples think Jesus is talking about? (verse 16)

f. In verse 18, Jesus highlights the hardness of their hearts by asking if they embody what three deficiencies?

1. In verses 19-20, why do you think Jesus makes the disciples answer how many leftovers were collected from the miraculous feedings? What is Jesus doing here? What is going on?

2. Could Jesus also say of us, "How is it you do not understand?" What things has He done for us that we so easily forget or forsake? Discuss.

3. Read Matthew 23:1-12.

   a. What sentence best describes the theme of this whole passage? (verse 5)

b. What things do we do in our church culture to be seen? How big a problem is this? What can we do about it?

c. Jesus specifies that we should call no man Rabbi, father, or teacher. What are His reasons for forbidding that?

d. What terms do we bestow on people today that should only be reserved for God?

4. Read Luke 11:14-23.

a. In verse 23, Jesus draws a hard line here when it comes to following Him. Why do we allow the world to cast Jesus as a moderate teacher who claimed no divinity?

b. Would verse 23 be a good tool to evangelize people with? Why or why not?

5. What has this study of Jesus' miracles in the section of Mark taught you and showed you about the Savior that you never knew or realized before?

DID YOU KNOW?

The Gospel of Mark has many distinctions attributed to it. Of the four Gospels, scholars have surmised that Mark was written first and was used as original source material for the Gospels of Matthew and Luke. There are many interesting details found in Mark that are not seen in any other of the other Gospel accounts. Only Mark specifically refers to Herod as the king during the time of Jesus' ministry (Mark 6:14, 24). Only in Mark is Jesus referred to as a carpenter (Mark 6:3). And only Mark gives us the very important historical detail that the Mount of Olives sat across from the temple (Mark 13:3), a fact that can be verified in Jerusalem even today.

ADDITIONAL RESOURCES
by Dr. David Jeremiah

A.D. THE REVOLUTION THAT CHANGED THE WORLD

In *A.D. The Revolution That Changed the World,* Dr. David Jeremiah takes us on a voyage through the life of the apostles after Christ's resurrection. Following the life of Stephen, Paul, Peter, and others, Dr. Jeremiah shows us that these apostles not only shared the Good News but continued to fight for their faith despite persecution, adversity, and rebellion. This book holds within it the action-packed struggles and successes that led to the formation of the Early Church.

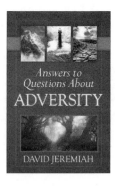

ANSWERS TO QUESTIONS ABOUT ADVERSITY

Adversity comes in all shapes and sizes and is no respecter of persons here on earth. We've all wondered, "Why is this happening to me?" and this book is meant to answer just that. In a question-and-answer format, Dr. David Jeremiah answers questions like "Does everyone struggle with temptation?" and "Why does God allow pain?" so that we might get a better understanding of the reasons we face adversity and develop the strategies to move past our pain.

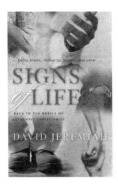

SIGNS OF LIFE

Just as a hospital patient is checked for "vital signs" of life, we must also check our signs of life in the Body of Christ. We're to reflect authenticity, generosity, and compassion daily, just as Christ did. These *Signs of Life* are public expressions of our private faith; and through our words and acts of kindness, we can make an impact on unsaved lives. This book will help us better understand what it means to be a Christian so that we can share our faith to the fullest.

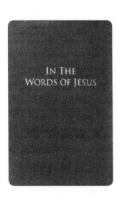

IN THE WORDS OF JESUS

Do not be anxious for tomorrow. . . Love your enemies. . . Go and sin no more. . . The words of Jesus are unlike any other. He has rescued sinners and lifted the spirits of multitudes throughout time, and His phrases and metaphors have shaped world opinion. *In the Words of Jesus* contains some of the most important statements He made so that we can reflect on what He said and apply it to our lives every day.

Each of these resources was created from a teaching series by Dr. David Jeremiah. Contact Turning Point for more information about correlating materials.

For pricing information and ordering, contact us at

P.O. Box 3838
San Diego, CA 92163
(800) 947-1993
www.DavidJeremiah.org

STAY CONNECTED
to Dr. David Jeremiah

Take advantage of two great ways to let Dr. David Jeremiah give you spiritual direction every day!

Turning Points Magazine and Devotional

Receive Dr. David Jeremiah's magazine, *Turning Points*, each month:

- Thematic study focus
- 48 pages of life-changing reading
- Relevant articles
- Special features
- Daily devotional readings
- Bible study resource offers
- Live event schedule
- Radio & television information

Request *Turning Points* magazine today!

(800) 947-1993
www.DavidJeremiah.org/Magazine

Daily Turning Point E-Devotional

Start your day off right! Find words of inspiration and spiritual motivation waiting for you on your computer every morning! Receive a daily e-devotion communication from David Jeremiah that will strengthen your walk with God and encourage you to live the authentic Christian life.

Request your free e-devotional today!

(800) 947-1993
www.DavidJeremiah.org/Devo